eland

Enjoy Cleveland!

101 THINGS TO DO IN CLEVELAND

Gary J. Sikorski

Other Schiffer Books by the Author:
101 Things to Do in Martha's Vineyard, ISBN: 978-0-7643-4953-9
101 Things to Do in Rhode Island, ISBN: 978-0-7643-5138-9
101 Things to Do in Key West, ISBN: 978-0-7643-5476-2

Library of Congress Control Number: 2025930650

Edited by Ian Robertson
Designed by Alexa Harris
Cover design by Alexa Harris
Type set in Cinzel / Times New Roman

ISBN: 978-0-7643-7023-6
ePub: 978-1-5073-0608-6
Printed in China

10 9 8 7 6 5 4 3 2 1

FSC
www.fsc.org
MIX
Paper | Supporting responsible forestry
FSC® C167893

Published by Schiffer Publishing, Ltd.
4880 Lower Valley Road
Atglen, PA 19310
Phone: (610) 593-1777; Fax: (610) 593-2002
Email: info@schifferbooks.com
Web: www.schifferbooks.com

CONTENTS

PREFACE

I am thrilled to say that this is my fourth book in what has turned into a very personally satisfying series of photographic guides written to share my insight on all the activities I have experienced in the different places I have lived. And I have lived in many, many different places over the years. This was all due to the fact that for a good portion of my time here on this earth, I was a seasonal waiter, gladly spending my winters in the South and my summers back in the touristy coastal towns up north. When I wasn't waiting tables (which was very profitable in these different seasonal locations), I was out exploring and experiencing all the activities each location had to offer. Each day was a new adventure, and I always took along my camera. My previous three books focused on some of the destinations where I had set up my seasonal residences, the first being Martha's Vineyard, the second, Rhode Island, and the third, Key West. This fourth book now brings to you the excitement of a place I am much more acquainted with than the previous three, and very excited to tell you about, and that is my hometown, Cleveland, Ohio. Born and raised in the suburbs of Cleveland, at one point owning a business in Ohio City, and now once again living in Cleveland, I have seen the city grow and develop over the past few decades. So much so that I knew this would be the time to add Cleveland to my catalog of exciting destination locations. And I'm so happy that my publisher agreed! I had a wonderful time revisiting the places that I've been to many times before and visiting the new and newly renovated spots to compile, photograph, and complete this work, of which I am so proud. It was a lot of work, but I had a blast. And I hope you have as much fun with my 101 suggestions of things to do as I have had bringing them to you.

WELCOME
Edgewater
A Premier Cleveland Neighborhood

Clevelander
Bar & Grill
SPIRITS
RAMIREZ
11

STARBOARD
Sprint

ACKNOWLEDGMENTS

It was such a joy creating this guide, but of course it would not have been possible to give life to this book without the assistance of so many friends, old and new, who helped me in some way along my journey. To all of you, I am so very grateful.

First, for their kind generosity, their contributive information, and providing some of their fantastic photography, I'd like to thank Ian Adams; Amanda Chambers at CityMusic; Rockell Churby-Llanos, Nina Domingue, and Roger Mastroianni at Karamu House; Andrew Keller with Video Game Symphony; William Pierce at Maltz Museum; Kim Furganson and Steve Wagner at Cleveland Public Theatre; Mike Tata and Evan Duly with the Cleveland Agora; Anthony Elder, Samantha Fryberger, and Amber Patrick at Cleveland Aquarium; Cindy Barber at the Beachland Ballroom; Bart Gabbard from the Bookhouse Brewery; Captain Rick Fryan and Cheryl Colicchio from the *Goodtime III*; Darren Thompson at the Bop Stop; and Dina Kostis from Hilarities 4th Street Theatre. I'm sure there are a few names that I have overlooked, and to those who may have contributed but were left off this list, my apologies.

I'd also like to thank Nancy Sikorski; Linda Dutkowski; my mom, Dolores Sikorski; Sheila and Peter Badal; Briana Weir; and Kim Bell for all their thoughtful suggestions. I am also very grateful to Xavier Bay and Arry Lazaridis of the Cleveland City Planning Commission for providing the maps found in this book. Most importantly, I would like to express my gratefulness and sincere thanks to Judy Courtemanche for her help in reviewing and proofreading my text. Your expertise and keen eye were invaluable and so appreciated!

Last, many thanks to Peter Schiffer for giving this project the green light; my editor, Ian Robertson, for all his hard work; and all the creative souls at Schiffer Publishing. Once again, everyone at Schiffer has been such a pleasure to work with. And as always, I am so pleased with the wonderful results of all your hard work.

Thank you all very, very much.

INTRODUCTION

If you haven't been to Cleveland lately, then you really haven't been to Cleveland. Each day brings another exciting improvement and new development, which brings continued enthusiasm and an increased sense of civic pride that can be seen and felt throughout all of northeastern Ohio. The remarkable growth and enhancement taking place in this vibrant lakeside city is reason enough for landing CLE on so many "must visit" destination lists. *Travel + Leisure* named Cleveland one of its fifty best places to travel in 2024, putting Cleveland in its "Big City Thrills" category. *The Points Guy* included CLE on its list of the sixteen best places to travel, remarking that the north coast city "just might be the hottest new cruise destination in North America," as Cleveland experienced a 700% increase in ship visits in just two years. As many people are finding out, there are now so many fantastic reasons to visit "The Land."

The city of Cleveland, a port city connected to the Atlantic Ocean via the Saint Lawrence Seaway, was founded in 1796 near the mouth of the Cuyahoga River, in the area known today as the Flats, by General Moses Cleaveland, a Revolutionary War veteran. The new town was named after its founder, but as rumor has it, the city's first newspaper dropped the "a" from the spelling to fit the name on its masthead. The city's prime geographic location on the river and the lakeshore made it ideal for industrial development, which attracted large numbers of immigrants looking for work. This influx of residents reached its peak in 1910, as Cleveland became the sixth-largest-populated city in the United States. It also attracted many of the wealthiest men in the world, who spent their fortunes creating many of CLE's wonderful cultural institutions, the most prominent being the Cleveland Museum of Art and the Cleveland Orchestra. The city flourished, being named an All-American City for the first time in 1949. By 1950 the population of the city of Cleveland was more than 900,000. But as manufacturing experienced a downturn in the 1960s and the economy began to slow, a good portion of the population moved out to the suburbs. The city entered a period of decline and started to suffer economically, a period that lasted for decades.

Today the city's remarkable transformation has put the past in the rearview mirror. Walk by the Guardians of Transportation and you'll find a city lined with a growing network of bike paths, parks, and trails; a culinary mecca surrounded by new hotels and trendy restaurants; a sports town that boasts the best sports fanatics on the planet; and a waterfront wonderland with activities for young and old alike. Colorful street art brightens up the thoroughfares, breweries and coffee shops are seemingly on every block, history can be found around every corner, and European flair can be found on almost every menu. You'll experience a modern city with midwestern hospitality bursting with a contagious energy from the warm and welcoming people of "The Land."

Cleveland is now on track to becoming one of America's great travel destinations, and the future of this amazing city couldn't be brighter. Hundreds of millions of dollars are earmarked for dozens of northeastern Ohio projects. The Rock & Roll Hall of Fame is expanding, the development of the Tower City Riverfront has begun, and a 25-acre park will soon grace Irishtown Bend along the Cuyahoga River. Ground has been broken for a new $250 million astronaut-training center. An estimated 3.5 million square feet of office space, residential living, commercial rental properties, and entertainment facilities along the Cuyahoga River will be available in the coming years. A master plan is underway to connect the city to the waterfront with new bike trails that will link Edgewater Park to the East 55th Street Marina. Canal Basin Park will be redesigned, and the Bridgeworks Project, focusing on redeveloping the major intersection of West 25th Street and the Detroit-Superior Bridge, is currently underway. For Cleveland the future has never looked brighter.

So turn the page and come along with *101 Things to Do in Cleveland* and discover many of the exciting things to see and do in this vibrant and beautiful city on the shores of Lake Erie.

A PERFECT DAY IN

CLEVELAND

I know you would love to experience my entire list of 101 things to do, but you might just be passing through, or you're in town on business and you have only one day to explore the CLE. With so much that our city has to offer, trying to put together a one-day itinerary on your own could be a daunting task, so I've attempted to do it for you. There are so many options from which to choose; too bad the days aren't a bit longer! And undoubtedly there is going to be a festival, concert, or special event you'll have to pencil in on your own. It wasn't easy putting together this one-day schedule, and due to time constraints I had to overlook many things not close to downtown, but here are my suggestions for that perfect day in Cleveland.

8:30 a.m.	Start your day off with a nice breakfast at either Karen Small's Juneberry Table or the Judith, a relative newcomer in Ohio City, or the long-standing Lucky's Café in Tremont.
10:00 a.m.	Time for a little sightseeing. Head on over to University Circle, known for its world-class museums and institutions. Start at the internationally renowned Cleveland Museum of Art. Then, if you have time, walk over to either the newly renovated Museum of Natural History or the Cleveland Botanical Garden. The garden's Costa Rica Glasshouse is a tropical retreat that really shouldn't be missed.
12:30 p.m.	To experience CLE, a stroll through the historic West Side Market is a must. It's also a great spot to grab some lunch. Pick out some meat, cheese, and a baguette or, better yet, just wander over to Frank's Bratwurst. I've been enjoying their bratwurst sandwich on a soft roll for over fifty years!
1:00 p.m.	Walk outside the market and you'll be surrounded by breweries. Grab a beer at the Market Garden Brewery, Hansa Brewery, or the Great Lakes Brewing Company. Cheers! And if you're with kids, walk on down to Mitchell's Homemade Ice Cream. It's early, so there might not be a line.
2:00 p.m.	Get ready to rock! Head downtown to the Rock & Roll Hall of Fame. I. M. Pei's glass pyramid has just been expanded, and of course this is one of the top attractions in town. If you're not ready to rock, head to the Great Lakes Science Center right next door.
4:00 p.m.	Right behind the rock hall and the science center is North Coast Harbor. Take a minute to pose in front of the iconic Cleveland Script sign on the inner harbor promenade. Great photo op. Then take a short stroll to Public Square. Get an up-close look at the Terminal Tower, poke your head inside the Soldier's and Sailors' Monument, and make a stop across the street to visit the Museum of Illusions. It's open late.
5:30 p.m.	Head on over to East 4th Street, lined with outdoor patios and some of CLE's best restaurants. You'll find a variety of options for a great meal. For a lavish dinner, Marble Room Steaks is around the corner.
7:30 p.m.	Time for some entertainment! You're on East 4th Street, so you could check out a comedy show at Hilarities or see what's happening at the House of Blues. If you planned ahead for tickets the nation's largest performing arts center outside New York City, the Playhouse Square District is just a few blocks away.
11:00 p.m.	End your night with a beverage along the Cuyahoga River in the Flats Entertainment District. For something a little more subdued, stop instead at the Velvet Tango Room for one of their handcrafted cocktails.

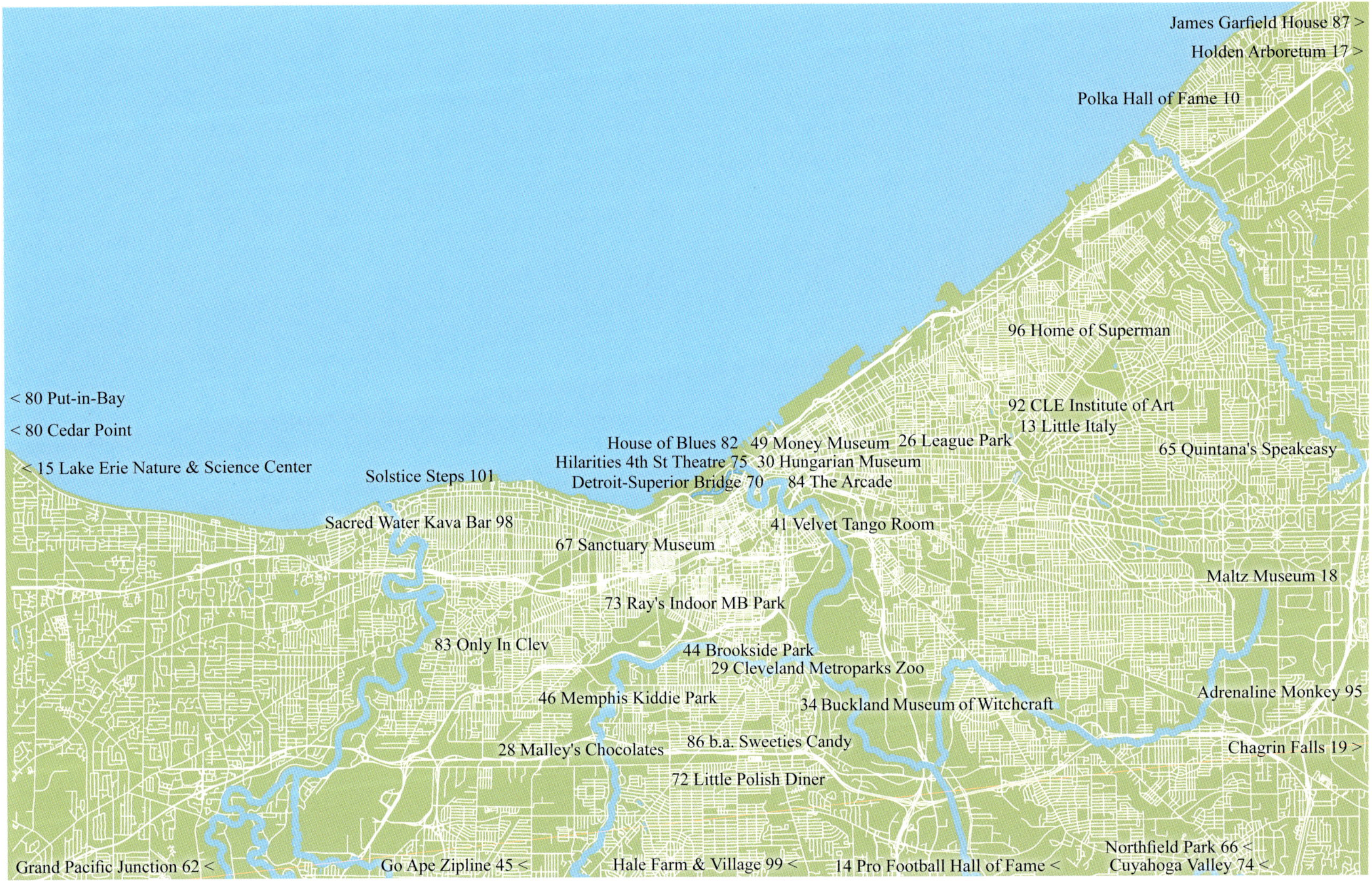
James Garfield House 87 >
Holden Arboretum 17 >
Polka Hall of Fame 10
96 Home of Superman
< 80 Put-in-Bay
< 80 Cedar Point
< 15 Lake Erie Nature & Science Center
92 CLE Institute of Art
13 Little Italy
House of Blues 82
49 Money Museum
26 League Park
65 Quintana's Speakeasy
Hilarities 4th St Theatre 75
30 Hungarian Museum
Solstice Steps 101
Detroit-Superior Bridge 70
84 The Arcade
Sacred Water Kava Bar 98
41 Velvet Tango Room
67 Sanctuary Museum
Maltz Museum 18
73 Ray's Indoor MB Park
83 Only In Clev
44 Brookside Park
29 Cleveland Metroparks Zoo
46 Memphis Kiddie Park
34 Buckland Museum of Witchcraft
Adrenaline Monkey 95
86 b.a. Sweeties Candy
28 Malley's Chocolates
Chagrin Falls 19 >
72 Little Polish Diner
Northfield Park 66 <
Grand Pacific Junction 62 <
Go Ape Zipline 45 <
Hale Farm & Village 99 <
14 Pro Football Hall of Fame <
Cuyahoga Valley 74 <

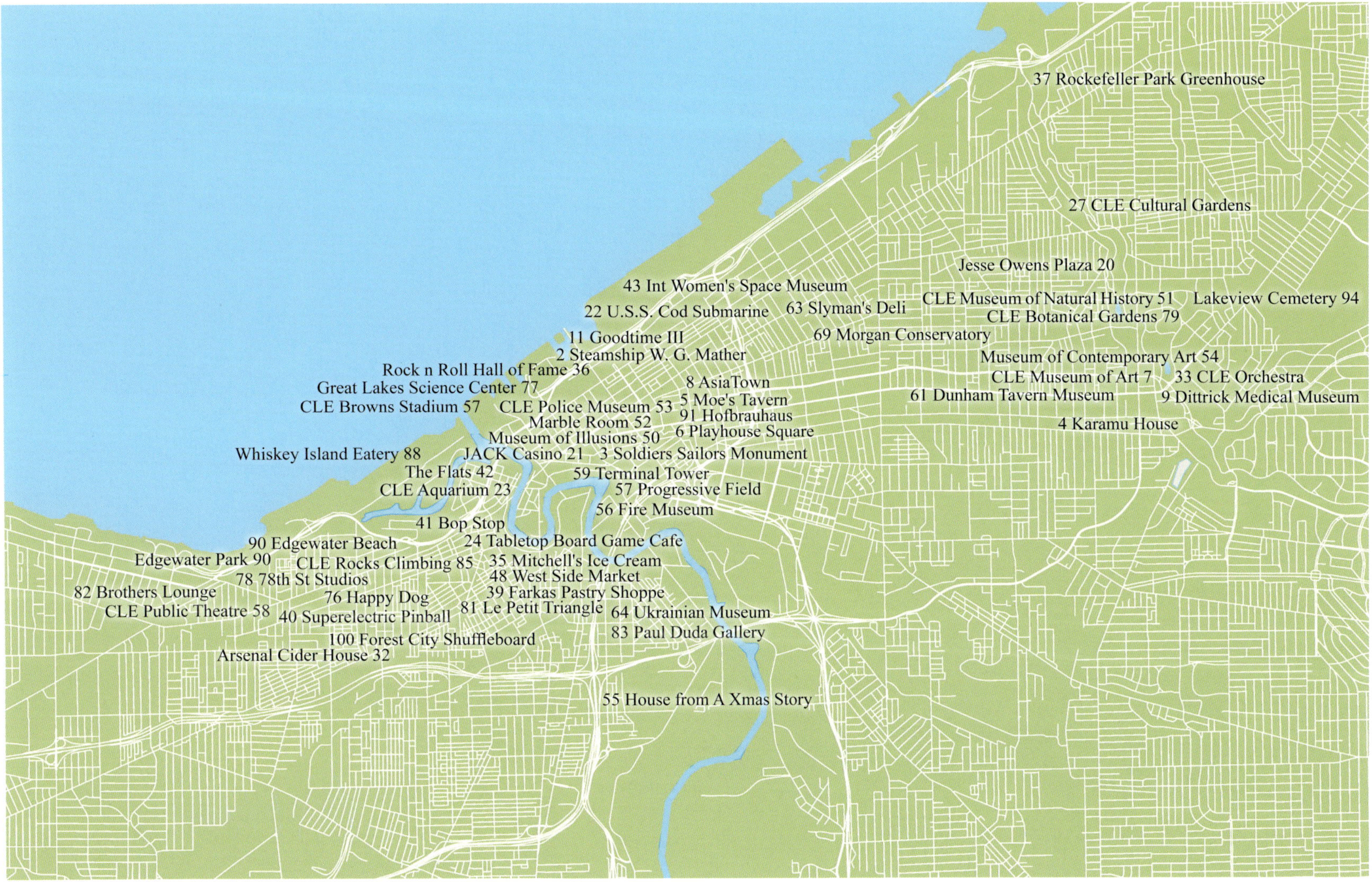
37 Rockefeller Park Greenhouse
27 CLE Cultural Gardens
Jesse Owens Plaza 20
43 Int Women's Space Museum
22 U.S.S. Cod Submarine
63 Slyman's Deli
CLE Museum of Natural History 51
Lakeview Cemetery 94
CLE Botanical Gardens 79
11 Goodtime III
69 Morgan Conservatory
2 Steamship W. G. Mather
Museum of Contemporary Art 54
Rock n Roll Hall of Fame 36
8 AsiaTown
CLE Museum of Art 7
33 CLE Orchestra
Great Lakes Science Center 77
5 Moe's Tavern
61 Dunham Tavern Museum
9 Dittrick Medical Museum
CLE Browns Stadium 57
CLE Police Museum 53
91 Hofbrauhaus
Marble Room 52
4 Karamu House
Museum of Illusions 50
6 Playhouse Square
Whiskey Island Eatery 88
JACK Casino 21
3 Soldiers Sailors Monument
The Flats 42
59 Terminal Tower
CLE Aquarium 23
57 Progressive Field
56 Fire Museum
41 Bop Stop
90 Edgewater Beach
24 Tabletop Board Game Cafe
Edgewater Park 90
CLE Rocks Climbing 85
35 Mitchell's Ice Cream
78 78th St Studios
48 West Side Market
82 Brothers Lounge
76 Happy Dog
39 Farkas Pastry Shoppe
CLE Public Theatre 58
40 Superelectric Pinball
81 Le Petit Triangle
64 Ukrainian Museum
100 Forest City Shuffleboard
83 Paul Duda Gallery
Arsenal Cider House 32
55 House from A Xmas Story

NO. 1

Discover CLE's rich history from 1796 to the present at the Cleveland History Center

Cleveland History Center
10825 East Blvd., University Circle | www.wrhs.org/plan-visit/places-to-visit/cleveland-history-center

Cleveland Starts Here! That's the mantra of this grand dame of a museum, which also serves as the headquarters of the Western Reserve Historical Society. The 9-acre complex is packed with a variety of collections and intriguing exhibits covering all aspects of the city's history, from founder Moses Cleaveland's 1796 pipe and tobacco pouch to Lebron James's sneakers worn during the 2016 championship season. Ride the restored Euclid Beach Carousel, walk through two historic mansions, explore two floors of vintage and classic automobiles, and marvel at the most comprehensive costume and textile collection in the country. Experience over two hundred years of Cleveland history; what a way to start!

LeBron James' Shoes
2016

NO. 2

Climb aboard the 618-foot Steamship *William G. Mather*, "The Ship That Built Cleveland"

Steamship *William G. Mather*
601 Erieside Avenue, Downtown | www.greatscience.com/explore/exhibits/william-g-mather-steamship

Take a stroll along Cleveland's beautifully renovated North Coast Harbor behind the Great Lakes Science Center and the Rock & Roll Hall of Fame and you won't be able to miss her. Transporting cargo such as ore, stone, and grain on the Great Lakes for fifty-five years, the steamship *William G. Mather* is now enjoying retirement as a floating museum. It's nicknamed "The Ship That Built Cleveland," and the terrific walking tour of the four-story vessel features the crew's cramped living quarters (and the captain's stately quarters), elegant guest staterooms, the brass-and-oak pilothouse, dining rooms and pantry, and the enormous engine room. And walking from bow to stern on the ship's deck, you'll find great views of the entire harbor.

NO. 3

Honor our local veterans who served in the Civil War at the Soldiers' and Sailors' Monument

Soldiers' and Sailors' Monument
3 Public Square, Downtown | www.soldiersandsailors.com

The Soldiers' and Sailors' Monument, standing proudly in the southeast quadrant of Public Square, is a stately Civil War monument saluting the nine-thousand-plus city residents who served the Union during the American Civil War. The exterior is surrounded by four remarkable bronze statues symbolizing the principal branches of the service: the Cavalry, the Infantry, the Navy, and the Artillery. Upon entering the interior, you'll be treated to a grand memorial tablet room, with the names of the Cuyahoga County Union soldiers carved into the marble walls. Step inside next time you're walking by!

NO. 4

Take in a play at Karamu House, the oldest producing Black theater in the nation

Karamu House Theatre
2355 East 89th Street, Fairfax | www.karamuhouse.org

One of Cleveland's greatest cultural treasures, Karamu House, established in 1915, is recognized nationally for its dedication to diverse theater while honoring the Black experience. Many of Langston Hughes's plays premiered at this theater. Spend a fantastic evening taking in one of their productions, which might include an American premiere or an award-winning Broadway show. In addition to thought-provoking plays, the theater also produces musicals, comedy shows, jazz performances, and poetry nights. You could also partake in their free community programs, such as line-dancing lessons, poetry workshops, African dance, musical concerts, and more!

Photo courtesy of Roger Mastroianni

NO. 5

Have a drink at Moe's Tavern, the inspiration for Moe's on *The Simpsons*

Moe's Tavern
1740 East 17th Street at Walnut Avenue, Downtown | www.moes-cle.com

Fact or fiction? We may never know, but supposedly Bill Morrison and Tone Rodriguez were young students who took a few classes at nearby Cleveland State University. While there, they shared a space in the old rooming house above Moe's Tavern, a dive bar they frequented to wet their whistles. Eventually the pair moved on to Hollywood and were hired as two of the early artists/illustrators/writers of *The Simpsons*. When Moe's was created for the popular TV series, allegedly the two used their old college hangout as the inspiration. Some give this honor to a local bar near Eugene, Oregon (Springfield on the TV show), but that Eugene Moe's Tavern didn't open until 2013, long after the show was created. I'm laying my money down on this friendly little spot off Walnut Avenue!

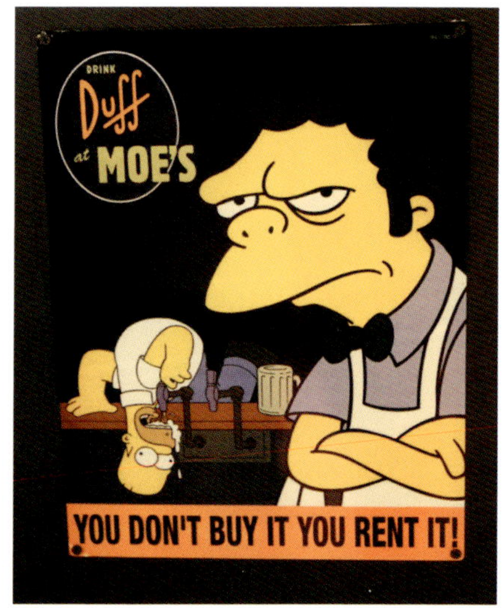

NO. 6

Experience the excitement of a Broadway show in the dazzling Playhouse Square Theater District

Playhouse Square Theater District
Centered along Euclid Avenue, between East 13th and East 17th Streets | www.playhousesquare.org

Lined with sparkling marquees and crowned with the world's largest outdoor chandelier, this vibrant entertainment district in downtown Cleveland is the nation's largest performing-arts center outside New York City. Visited by over one million people a year, Playhouse Square showcases five major 1920s-era theaters (the Allen, Connor Palace, Mimi Ohio, State, and Hanna) and several smaller performing-arts venues, along with restaurants, bars, offices, and nearby world-class hotels. Over one thousand shows take place in the district every year, including award-winning Broadway productions, musical and comedy acts, famous lecturers, and dance performances. The district is also home to resident companies such as the Cleveland Ballet and the Cleveland International Film Festival.

NO. 7

Savor the beauty of the artistic masterpieces at the world-renowned Cleveland Museum of Art

The Cleveland Museum of Art
11150 East Blvd., University Circle | www.clevelandart.org

Renowned for its superb quality and immensity of its collection, the Cleveland Museum of Art is the most visited art museum in the world. With more than 66,500 works of art spanning over 6,000 years of creativity, the internationally recognized galleries include decorative art, an Egyptian collection, European paintings and sculptures, Indigenous art, medieval art, western drawings, Greek and Roman art, a textile collection, and much more. Treasures by the likes of Matisse, Dalí, Renoir, Monet, Picasso, and Vincent van Gogh are on display. And unbelievably, there is never a fee to visit one of the greatest art museums on the planet!

NO. 8

Fall in love with the restaurants and Asian specialty shops in CLE's AsiaTown neighborhood

AsiaTown
East 30th Street to East 40th Street, from Perkins to St. Clair | www.asiatowncleveland.org

Formerly known as Chinatown, which occupied just a few blocks on Rockwell Avenue, AsiaTown has expanded into what has now become a wonderfully vibrant cultural destination. Primarily Chinese, Korean, and Vietnamese, this diverse Asian neighborhood is packed with lively businesses for blocks on end. A good start would be Asia Plaza, with plenty of interesting shops such as Ball Ball Waffle, serving authentic Hong Kong–style bubble waffles, and the perennial dim sum favorite eatery Li Wah. A few other not-to-be-missed locations are Koko Bakery, specializing in sweet- and savory-flavored steamed buns, AsiaTown Center, with an herbal store and a supermarket, and Superior Pho, an award-winning Vietnamese restaurant.

Xiang Ru
Tou Gu Cao
Song Piao Xiao
Si Gua Luo
Please Ask for Assistance

NO. 9

Examine the huge array of medical artifacts at the Dittrick Museum of Medical History

Dittrick Museum of Medical History
Case Western Reserve University, 11000 Euclid Avenue, University Circle | www.artsci.case.edu/dittrick/

From what started in 1898 as a collection of bygone medical devices in a small display cabinet in the Prospect Avenue home of the Cleveland Medical Library Association, the Dittrick Museum has grown into one of the most comprehensive collections of surgical instruments and medical equipment in all of America. During your physical examination of the more than 175,000 amazing artifacts, you'll find microscopes, nursing uniforms, historical contraceptive devices, turn-of-the-twentieth-century x-ray equipment, and an 1875 doctor's office. It's best to call ahead, since museum hours are limited.

NO. 10

Take three quick steps and a hop on your way to the Polka Hall of Fame

National Cleveland-Style Polka Hall of Fame
605 East 222nd Street, Euclid | www.clevelandstyle.com

Founded in 1987, this fantastic hall is dedicated to the preservation and promotion of the "happiest sound around" . . . polka music! Cleveland, with its strong Polish and eastern European heritage, has always been renowned as America's Polka Capital. Helping to cement that reputation was "the Slovenian kid from Collinwood," the legendary Frankie Yankovic. Lots of the Polka King's memorabilia is on display, along with accordions of many of the polka greats, their colorful stage outfits, original polka albums, and historic photographs. There is also a room dedicated to award-winning Polka Hall of Fame honorees. No doubt about it, Cleveland is still Polka Town USA!

NO. 11

Climb aboard the *Goodtime III* for a narrated sightseeing cruise down the Cuyahoga River

Goodtime III
825 East 9th Street Pier, North Coast Harbor | www.Goodtimeiii.com

What a fun and fantastic way to view the city! Hop aboard the thousand-passenger *Goodtime III* and head out on the water on board the largest sightseeing vessel on the Great Lakes. Take a comfy seat on any of the four decks and enjoy a wonderfully narrated tour of the Cuyahoga River and Lake Erie, passing patio decks packed with diners, bars, and nightclubs; riverside parks; attractive new apartment buildings and condos; fantastic views of the many bridges; and Cleveland's remarkable skyline. This third-generation cruising boat sails May through September and also offers luncheon, dinner, special-event, happy-hour, and sunset cruises.

GOODTIME III

NO. 12

Find peace through mutual understanding by roaming the Cleveland Cultural Gardens

Cleveland Cultural Gardens
Along MLK Jr. Drive & East Blvd., from I-90 to University Circle |
www.clevelandculturalgardens.org

Located in Rockefeller Park and weaving for almost 2 miles, the Cleveland Cultural Gardens are a wonderful collection of thirty-six public gardens all designed, cultivated, and maintained by distinct cultural or nationality communities of Cleveland. Using sidewalks, bordered paths, and connecting stone staircases, you'll stroll by plants and trees native to each garden's home country, decorative waterfalls, and more than eighty busts, statues, and monuments of poets, philosophers, composers, scientists, and others that express the cultural pride of each ethnic group.

IMMIGRANT MOTHER

No. 13

Stroll down the sidewalks of Little Italy, lined with old-school Italian eateries, bakeries, and shops

Little Italy
Mayfield Road, between East 119th Street and East 125th Street | www.littleitalycle.com

A little pasta, a little vino, a strong espresso, and a nice cigar. There's nothing like a night out on Mayfield Road in Little Italy, the main thoroughfare crammed with elegant trattorias, art galleries, pizzerias, wine shops, and bakeries. The sounds of friendly chatter and street musicians fill the air for blocks in this historic neighborhood formed in the mid-1800s, when Italian immigrants settled in this area to work for Italian sculptor Joseph Carrabelli. When visiting, be sure to check out the Italian American Museum of Cleveland to learn about the heritage and history of CLE's Italian American community.

BAKERY
PRESTI'S
ITALIAN PASTRY
PRESTI'S BAKERY
ONE WAY
Mazz's
12113
Murray H

NO. 14

Pay homage to the most popular sport in America at the Pro Football Hall of Fame

Pro Football Hall of Fame
2121 George Halas Drive NW, Canton | www.profootbalhof.com

Only an hour's drive from the CLE, the Pro Football Hall of Fame is an experience that should not be missed. Opened in 1963, this unbelievable shrine is packed with exhibits, memorabilia, artifacts, jerseys, signatures, photographs, and so much more. The main attraction, the Hall of Fame Gallery, proudly displays over three hundred bronze busts of the legends who have been honored with enshrinement, while the Super Bowl Gallery, with collectibles from every championship game, occasionally showcases the iconic Lombardi Trophy.

HALL
FAME
CINTAS

No. 15

Get an up-close look at hawks, snakes, and owls at the Lake Erie Nature & Science Center

Lake Erie Nature & Science Center
28728 Wolf Road, Bay Village | www.lensc.org

Tucked away on the Cleveland Metroparks's Huntington Reservation in Bay Village is a surprisingly wonderful little nature center. Up-close encounters with hawks, bald eagles, crows, snakes, turtles, and aquariums stocked with Lake Erie fish species are all brilliantly displayed both in their indoor and outdoor exhibits. And for a terrific experience, take a seat in the center's planetarium, one of two public-access planetariums in Cuyahoga County, with sixteen public stargazing opportunities every week.

NO. 16

Attend a Video Game Symphony concert by one of the world's only orchestras dedicated to video game music

Video Game Symphony
Various locations throughout NE Ohio | www.videogamesymphony.com

Talk about bringing the joy! This masterful, all-volunteer ensemble is one of the only professional-caliber orchestras in the world dedicated exclusively to performing the glorious music of video games. With more than sixty-five orchestra members and a choir, they are all doing it for the love of this music, and they're bringing it to you free of charge! So grab the kids and sit back and listen to electrifying performances of classic video game hits such as *Pokemon*, *Kingdom Hearts*, *Zelda*, the rousing main theme to *Super Mario Bros. Brawl*, or the theme to *Star Wars*. Bravo! Bravo indeed!

NO. 17

Explore the sprawling gardens, trails, ponds, and forests at the massive Holden Arboretum

Holden Arboretum
9550 Sperry Road, Kirkland | www.holdenfg.org

Established in 1931, the Holden Forests & Gardens has blossomed into one of the largest arboretums and botanical gardens in the country. Situated east of Cleveland on 3,600 stunning acres in Lake and Geauga Counties, this nature lover's paradise is packed with miles of winding trails and paths. Spend the day strolling through specialized gardens and ridge-lined woodlands and past bogs and ponds teeming with wildlife. Venture into the forest and walk the elevated Murch Canopy, climb to the top of the Kalberer Emergent Tower, and finish your visit relaxing at Meditation Point.

Photo courtesy of Ian Adams

NO. 18

Show your respect for all humanity at Maltz Museum of Jewish Heritage

Maltz Museum of Jewish History
2929 Richmond Road, Beachwood | www.maltzmuseum.org

Opened in 2005, Maltz Museum does an extraordinary job of celebrating the history of the Jewish community of greater Cleveland and northeastern Ohio. Touching and uplifting stories of Jewish immigrants are told through state-of-the-art interactives, films, documents, exhibits, and personal accounts. The showpiece in the museum is the remarkable Temple-Tifereth Israel gallery, where you'll find historic treasures, documents of antiquity, scrolls, and ritual objects. There's so much to learn and so much to feel, all while gaining a valuable understanding of Jewish customs and traditions.

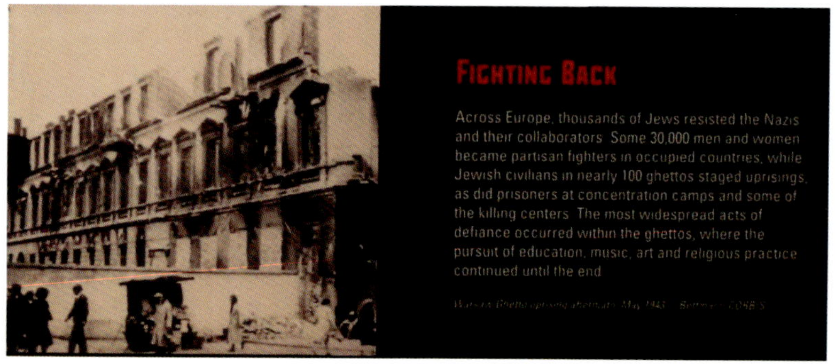

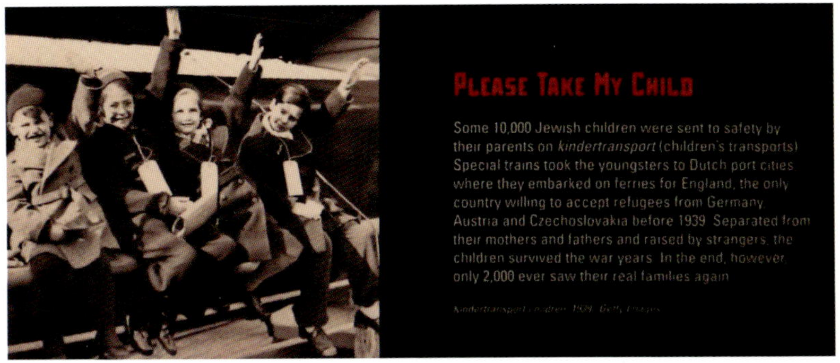
PLEASE TAKE MY CHILD
Some 10,000 Jewish children were sent to safety by their parents on *kindertransport* (children's transports). Special trains took the youngsters to Dutch port cities where they embarked on ferries for England, the only country willing to accept refugees from Germany, Austria and Czechoslovakia before 1939. Separated from their mothers and fathers and raised by strangers, the children survived the war years. In the end, however, only 2,000 ever saw their real families again.

Lamentations
Theodore Herzl
First Aliyah
International
Cleveland

1889 HEBREW OBSERVER
1964 CLEVELAND JEWISH NEWS
THE CLEVELAND PLAIN DEALER
ON THE RECORD
JEWISH NEWSPAPERS READ IN CLEVELAND
MENTOR
McCALL
THE JEWISH INDEPENDENT

NO. 19

Admire the spectacular waterfall, grab some popcorn, and stroll the quaint village of Chagrin Falls

Village of Chagrin Falls
North Main Street, Chagrin Falls | www.chagrin-falls-ohio.com

Only thirty-five minutes from downtown CLE, this charming village, with the Chagrin River running right through the center of town, has three historic districts on the National Register of Historic Places. This great little walking town has it all: a quaint downtown lined with boutiques and shops, swanky restaurants and bistros, a beautiful park, a historic popcorn shop stuffed floor to ceiling with nostalgic candies and treats, and a roaring waterfall surrounded by viewing decks. You'll want to visit the Fireside Book Shop, the original Dave's Cosmic Subs, and the popular Jeni's Splendid Ice Creams and then cap the evening off at the Chagrin Valley Little Theatre, one of the oldest community theaters in the country.

EVERGREEN
jenis
JodiDoesHair

NO. 20

Run the loop around Jesse Owens Olympic Oak Plaza, honoring track and field's greatest athlete

Jesse Owens Olympic Oak Plaza
Martin Luther King Jr. Drive, University Circle | www.universitycircle.org/jesse-owens-olympic-oak-plaza

Honoring James Cleveland "Jesse" Owens, the hometown legend considered the greatest and most famous track-and-field athlete of all time, Jesse Owens Olympic Oak Plaza circles around a single oak tree planted on Arbor Day 2021. The tree was propagated from one of the four trees awarded to Jesse for his four gold medals at the 1936 Olympic Games in Berlin. Take some time to walk or run around the 200-meter track encircling the plaza, decorated with four informative markers, one for each of Jesse's gold medals. The plaza also includes a colorful podium seat wall built to evoke the idea of a winner's stand.

NO. 21

Roll the dice, play the slots, and find yourself in the money at JACK Cleveland Casino

JACK Cleveland Casino
100 Public Square, Downtown | www.jackentertainment.com/cleveland

It could be your lucky day! Located in the building that once housed the iconic Higbee Department Store, the JACK Cleveland Casino in the Terminal Tower on Public Square is the place to lay down a couple of bucks. The huge complex sparkles with 1,200 slot machines, over one hundred blackjack and roulette tables, a twenty-eight-table poker room, a massive sports book that has a table games pit, and many other games of chance. It's a really lively way to spend the night with a chance of winning some extra cash. And look at it this way . . . you're in Cleveland, so it's already your lucky day!

NO. 22

Climb down the hatch and dive into naval history at the USS *Cod* Submarine Memorial

USS *Cod* Submarine Memorial
1201 North Marginal Road, Downtown | www.usscod.org

Officially launched on March 21, 1943, the USS *Cod* submarine now rests along the shores of Lake Erie just off East 9th Street. This 312-foot-long National Historical Landmark was awarded seven battle stars for her service in WWII, and she's credited with sinking more than twelve enemy vessels. Jump aboard and explore the upper deck, then climb down the forward torpedo room hatch and get ready to be amazed! The ship is historically intact, and you'll wander through the engine room and crew's quarters, pass by the radio room and kitchen, and marvel at the attack center. Onshore is a 2,806-pound submarine propeller, a working Cold War–era periscope, and a 3,000-pound Mark 14 torpedo.

224
U.S.S. COD

Photo courtesy of Amber Patrick, Greater Cleveland Aquarium

NO. 23

Get an up-close look at sharks and other sea creatures at Greater Cleveland Aquarium

Greater Cleveland Aquarium
2000 Sycamore Street, the Flats | www.greaterclevelandaquarium.com

Imagine great sand tiger sharks cruising silently over your head, giant Pacific octopi seemingly trying to wrap their arms around you, and stingrays whirling by so close you can reach out and touch them. You can experience all of this at Greater Cleveland Aquarium, housed in the historic Powerhouse building on the west bank of the Flats. Sea dragons, poison dart frogs, spotted garden eels, and chocolate chip sea stars are just a few of the 1,300 freshwater and saltwater animals from around the world that can be found in the aquarium's seven galleries.

NO. 24

Spend an evening playing as many games as you like at the Tabletop Board Game Café

Tabletop Board Game Café
1810 West 25th Street, Ohio City | www.tabletopcleve.com

With a game library featuring more than a thousand board games, the Tabletop Board Game Café makes for a perfect place to get together with friends, or to meet some new ones. Grab a seat in the bright and airy space surrounded by shelves that are filled with many of the classic games we loved as kids, as well as some of the newer, complicated strategy games. For just five bucks you can stay all night and play as many games as your heart desires. There's a small bar with an adjoining kitchen that offers sandwiches, gourmet snacks, shakes, coffee, beer, and wine. There's no Wi-Fi, so just sit back and enjoy the company and the competition.

NO. 25

Download Destination Cleveland's Brewery Passport and enjoy the beer at CLE's finest breweries

Destination Cleveland's Brewery Passport
334 Euclid Avenue, Downtown | www.thisiscleveland.com/things-to-do/experiences-tours/passports/cleveland-brewery-passport

It's no secret, as Destination Cleveland mentions on their website, but this town just really loves a good beer. And if you want to discover the best of CLE's beer makers, you need to download the Convention and Visitors Bureau's app. Check in at breweries such as Great Lakes, Bookhouse Brewing, Noble Beast, Immigrant Son, Market Garden Brewery, or the Jolly Scholar and earn points and win prizes. While there, look into the brewery tours that are offered at many of the beer-producing facilities. Beer made in Cleveland; it doesn't get much better than that!

You'll Prefer
NOBLE
BEAST
The Special
BEER

drunk BEER
made in
CLEVELAND

OKTOBERFEST 2019
GREAT AMERICAN BEER FESTIVAL 2019
MURDER BALLADS BALTIC PORTER
GREAT AMERICAN BEER FESTIVAL 2020
MURDER BALLADS BALTIC PORTER
2021
EVIL MOTIVES
TEUTONIC DISTORTION
OHIO

GREAT LAKES
BREWING Co
EST. 1988 CLEVELAND, OH

NO. 26

Take a swing at Cleveland's historic League Park and the Baseball Heritage Museum

League Park and the Baseball Heritage Museum
6601 Lexington Avenue, Hough | www.baseballheritagemuseum.org

Cleveland's historic League Park opened on May 1, 1891, with the legendary Cy Young pitching the Cleveland Spiders on to victory. Baseball's first grand slam was hit here in 1920 by the Cleveland Indian's Elmer Smith. Babe Ruth hit his five hundredth home run here in 1929, and the Cleveland Buckeyes won the 1945 Negro World Series on this field. The park's original ticket office has been restored and now houses the Baseball Heritage Museum. Packed with photos, programs, uniforms, and a treasure trove of game-used memorabilia, it remarkably captures the heart and soul of our nation's pastime.

NEW YORK CUBAN STARS
THE NEGRO LEAGUES
Cleveland
BUCKEYES
Newark
MONARCHS
PHILA STARS
KC
Cleveland Buckeyes 1945
Championship Infield
BASEBALL

On June 7, 1928, this ball was hit by Babe Ruth out of League Park, and retrieved by Connie Long. Babe signed the ball for Connie. Bill Long subsequently added other baseball legends' autographs.
Ball on loan from William Long.

NO. 27

Take a spin on the extensively restored Euclid Beach Park Grand Carousel

Euclid Beach Carousel
10825 East Blvd., University Circle | www.wrhs.org/explore/exhibits/euclid-beach-park-grand-carousel/

Many Clevelanders can still remember when these colorful, hand-carved wooden horses were the crown jewel of Euclid Beach Park on Cleveland's lakefront. The summer resort closed down in 1969, when the classic carousel was sold and shipped out of town. But it made a triumphant return in 2014. Lovingly restored by Carousel Works in Mansfield, the jumpers and golden chariots are once again open to the public in the Carousel Pavilion in the Cleveland History Center. So come on down, jump on a pony, and give it a whirl!

NO. 28

Indulge in some legendary sweet treats at Malley's Chocolates, Cleveland's premier chocolatiers

Malley's Chocolates
Eighteen locations throughout NE Ohio | www.malleys.com

Talk about your childhood wishes! Well, if those are fond memories, good times, and delicious chocolates, then you're probably talking about Cleveland's acclaimed confectioner Malley's Chocolates. This family-run business opened in 1935, and they are still churning out their original Pecan BillyBobs, scrumptious chocolate-covered pretzels, and iconic CLE chocolate bars. The family has eighteen stores throughout northeastern Ohio, but make it a point to visit the Lakewood, Mentor, or North Olmsted locations, where you can sit down at an old-fashioned soda fountain counter. Yummy!

NO. 29

Feed the giraffes and pet the goats at the Cleveland Metroparks Zoo & Rainforest

Cleveland Metroparks Zoo & Rain Forest
3900 Wildlife Way, Brookside Park | www.clevelandmetroparks.com/zoo

With more than 1.2 million visitors annually, the Cleveland Metroparks Zoo remains one of CLE's top attractions. The 183-acre indoor/outdoor wildlife park is teeming with over six hundred species of animals. Exhibits such as the Australian Adventure, African Elephant Crossing, Northern Wilderness Trek, and the Primate, Cat, and Aquatics habitats will keep the kids busy for an entire day. Although it charges a separate admission, the 2-acre, two-level Rainforest, with over six hundred animals from the jungles of Asia, Africa, and the Americas, should not be missed. However you decide to spend your day, don't leave without spending the extra three bucks to feed the giraffes!

NO. 30

Explore the folk costumes and unique artistry at the Cleveland Hungarian Museum

Cleveland Hungarian Museum
1301 East 9th Street in the Galleria at Erieview | www.clevelandhungarianmuseum.org

Walk through the ornately hand-carved "Szekely kapu" wooden gate; you're about to experience the rich history of the Hungarian community in northeastern Ohio. Lovingly preserved by the Cleveland Hungarian Heritage Society, the colorful collection includes beautifully decorated folk costumes, historical memorabilia, decorative pottery, Hungarian paintings and prints, a fascinating selection of Hungarian dolls, embroideries, and a library with over eight thousand books. Check out the gift shop before you leave, stocked with unique items including clothing, dolls, arts and crafts, decorative pillows, cookbooks, and paprika products. And unbelievably, admission is free!

NO. 31

Enjoy a chef-prepared meal while sightseeing on the water aboard the *Lady Caroline*

Lady Caroline
1153 Main Avenue, West Bank of the Flats | www.ladycaroline.com

If you would like to sail with a bit of luxury, the *Lady Caroline* might be just what you are looking for. Docked just up the river from Jacobs Pavilion and right beside the historic Powerhouse, this 120-foot-long dining cruise ship is one of the north coast's newest attractions. Setting sail for the first time in 2023, the *Lady Caroline* doesn't offer sightseeing excursions per se but, rather, specializes in chef-prepared lunch, brunch, and dinner cruises. The ship has three fully enclosed and climate-controlled decks and an open-sky deck complete with a covered bar and features onboard entertainment with a large dance floor.

NO. 32

Ride along with a local comedian and laugh your butt off on the Funny Bus Cleveland

Funny Bus Cleveland
1250 Old River Road, East Bank of the Flats | www.funnybus.net

The Funny Bus Cleveland, a hilarious ninety-minute trip on a fancy old school bus, is hosted by a local comedian, and it's BYOB. That's right, feel free to bring along a few adult beverages and get ready to laugh. This unique one-of-a-kind tour is of course comical, but it is also scenic (as you travel throughout downtown CLE, Ohio City, and Tremont) and informative (as you'll learn a little about nearby neighborhoods and the area's history). So sit back and experience all the action from your windowless seat as you heckle the comedian while you are being heckled by the people walking by.

NO. 33

Enjoy an extraordinary concert by the Cleveland Orchestra, one of the finest orchestras in the world

The Cleveland Orchestra
Severance Music Center, 11001 Euclid Avenue, University Circle | www.clevelandorchestra.com

Seeing the one-hundred-plus members of the world-renowned Cleveland Orchestra, regarded as one of the greatest orchestras in the world, is a magical experience that we are so blessed to be afforded here in the Land. And to put a cherry on top of the cake, their classical musical performances are held at majestic Severance Hall, regarded by music lovers as one of the most beautiful concert halls on the planet. It's a match made in heaven! When not performing in their University Circle home or traveling the world, the orchestra can be found playing at Blossom Music Center during the summer months, or performing free shows (such as the one pictured above at the Great Lakes Science Center) throughout the Greater Cleveland area.

NO. 34

Become spellbound by the extraordinary collections at Buckland Museum of Witchcraft & Magick

Buckland Museum of Witchcraft & Magick
2155 Broadview Road, Old Brooklyn |
www.bucklandmuseum.org

Founded by Ray Buckland in 1966, this fascinating gallery is the first and only museum in the United States to celebrate witchcraft and the occult. Enter through a colorful gift shop stacked floor to ceiling with magical supplies and souvenirs, and you'll find exhibits and Buckland's collection of artifacts procured from many of the notable leaders of the pagan and occult community. Ancient Egyptian funerary figurines, artifacts from the Salem Witch trials, Sybil Leek's crystal ball, Buckland's ritual robe, and hundreds of other bewitching items await. Drop in for a spell!

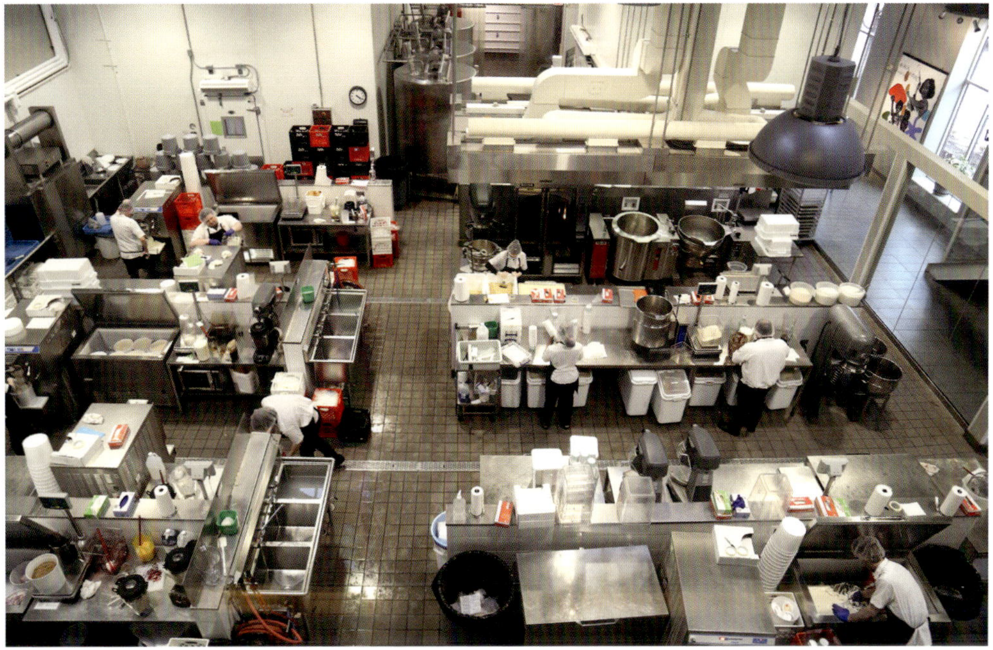

NO. 35

Stand in line for a "scoop of a smile in a cone" at Mitchell's Homemade Ice Cream

Mitchell's Homemade Ice Cream
1867 West 25th Street, Ohio City | www.mitchellshomemade.com

Don't let the ever-present queue leading into this grandiose ice cream parlor deter you; the Mitchell brothers keep the counter well staffed with smiling faces, and the line moves fast! Once inside their flagship location in Ohio City, filled with the delightful aroma of freshly made waffle cones, you'll need to choose from delicious choices such as blue cosmo, wildberry crumble, or peanut butter chocolate pretzel yogurt. Take your treat up to the second floor, where the huge windows give you a bird's-eye view of the 6,000-square-foot production kitchen in action.

NO. 36

Immerse yourself in musical history at the iconic Rock & Roll Hall of Fame

Rock & Roll Hall of Fame
1100 Rock & Roll Blvd., Downtown | www.rockhall.com

There's no doubt about it, Cleveland is the rock 'n' roll capital of the world. Celebrated CLE DJ Alan Freed introduced the term in his WJW radio studio just a few blocks away, and now his immortal microphone is one of the attractions here in I. M. Pei's glass-and-steel pyramid. Start on the bottom level, which features the stories of rock's earliest pioneers, along with tributes to today's emerging musicians. Eventually you'll work your way up to the Inductee Signature Gallery, where the Ramones, the Beatles, Elvis, the Rolling Stones, Bruce Springsteen, and other inductees' signatures are glimmering in gold. And thanks to KeyBank's generous $10 million gift, the hall offers free admission to residents of Cleveland.

INDUCTION MOMENTS

FURRY LEWIS
MEMPHIS
The Blues

ROCK&ROLL HALL OF FAME

LONG LIVE ROCK
ROCK & ROLL HALL OF FAME
2024 NOMINEE
DAVE MATTHEWS BAND
ROCK & ROLL HALL OF FAME
INDUCTION 2024
ROCK & ROLL HALL OF FAME
UNIONHOME
PLAZA

NO. 37

Relax among the exotic and native plants at the Rockefeller Park Greenhouse

Rockefeller Park Greenhouse & Botanical Garden
750 East 88th Street, University Circle | www.rockefellerparkgreenhouse.org

With so many popular sites in and around University Circle, you don't want to overlook this stunning greenhouse. Open seven days a week, year-round, with free admission, something is always in bloom in one of their specialty plant collections or colorful themed gardens. Highlights include a soothing Japanese Garden, the Willott Iris Garden (packed with award-winning irises), a Latin American Garden showcasing cacti and tropical fruit plants, and the Betty Ott Talking Garden, a sensory garden designed for the blind and featuring braille signage and audio descriptions. For a bit of a respite, bring along a book and enjoy the tranquility!

NO. 38

Trek the Towpath Trail, the amazing 101-mile pathway that follows the route of the Ohio & Erie Canal

Ohio & Erie Canal Towpath Trail
101 miles from CLE to New Philadelphia |
www.ohioanderiecanalway.com

Enjoy the great outdoors while following a path of history by transversing the Ohio & Erie Canal Towpath Trail. This historic trail was used from 1827 to 1913 by mules pulling canal boats along the banks. Today the recreational path is a marvel for walkers, joggers, and cyclists alike. Beginning at Canal Basin Park in downtown CLE, the trail winds along the Cuyahoga River, working its way through CLE's industrial valley, then past fields of wildflowers, scenic wetlands, and majestic forests as it heads south toward Canal Lands Park in New Philadelphia. Stretching your legs on the Tremont segment of the trail or biking down to the Peninsula Depot both are great ways to spend any afternoon!

TOWPATH TRAIL NORTH
CANAL BASIN PARK
CLEVELAND FOUNDATION
CENTENNIAL TRAIL
LAKE LINK

ROUNDHOUSE
The Roundhouse

NO. 39

Follow the aroma into Farkas Pastry Shoppe and indulge on their creamy "Old World" napoleons

Farkas Pastry Shoppe
2700 Lorain Avenue, Ohio City | www.farkaspastries.com

This shop was founded in 1966 by Hungarian refugee Sandor Farkas and his son Attila, and the tradition of making fine European pastries has been carried on after their passing by new owner Mike Harrison. Sandor's signature Hungarian kreme, or what we call napoleons, is the crowd favorite. But don't overlook the other specialties such as their elegant buttercream tortes, Hungarian dobos, or buttery linzers. This quaint shoppe is real old school, with a wide-open kitchen to watch everything being created. It's a wonderful stop on your way to the West Side Market!

NO. 40

Become a Pinball Wizard with the all-you-can-play arcade games at Superelectric Pinball Parlor

Superelectric Pinball Parlor
6500 Detroit Avenue, Gordon Square | www.superelectric.tv

Bells, knocks, chimes, clacks, and dings! Open the door to the parlor and you'll be hit with a wall of flashing color and those delightful sounds from the days of old. Pinball is back, and it's celebrated with an "all you can play for six bucks" glorification at Superelectric Pinball Parlor. The room is filled with pinball machines from the '50s to today's latest releases, with choices such as *Jaws*, *Bride of Pinbot*, *Iron Maiden*, and *Foo Fighters*. Grab a beverage at their cool little bar and go for that high score!

NO. 41

Tap into the pure inspiration of soulful jazz music at the BOP STOP or the Velvet Tango Room

BOP STOP at the Music Settlement
2920 Detroit Avenue, Hingetown District of Ohio City | www.themusicsettlement.org/bop-stop

Unfortunately there aren't as many places to see great live jazz performances as there used to be, but luckily there is one major venue that jazz connoisseurs can still count on for a great night out. The BOP STOP, nestled in the northwest corner of Ohio City, hosts over three hundred new and well-established jazz performances throughout the year. The intimate space is operated by the Music Settlement, a centuries-old community music school whose goal is to bring affordable music instruction to Cleveland's youth. And how cool is the BOP STOP? Well, the website All About Jazz named our intimate listening room one of the "Best Jazz Venues in the United States."

Velvet Tango Room
2095 Columbus Road, Duck Island |
www.velvettangoroom.com

A swanky room framed in dark mahogany, scarlet leather couches to sink your tush into, and sophisticated cocktails that are individually handcrafted to perfection. A baby grand piano squeezed into the corner and another piano in the hidden speakeasy behind a secret doorway. New York City, you might wonder? Chicago perhaps? Nope, it's CLE's own Velvet Tango Room. While there are so few options for a jazz-infused evening of entertainment, it's a blessing that this dimly lit club is still going strong. Enjoy live jazz duos, trios, or quartets on the weekends in the main room, and pianists in the speakeasy all week long.

NO. 42

Eat, drink, dance, and party along the Cuyahoga River in the bustling Cleveland Flats

The Flats
Along the Cuyahoga River, Downtown | www.thisiscleveland.com/blog/welcome-to-the-flats

Lining both sides of the winding Cuyahoga River, this low-lying area has emerged as one of the Midwest's premier entertainment districts. Thanks in part to a $750 million waterfront redevelopment project, the Flats is now home to boutique hotels, high-end residences, swanky restaurants, wonderful breweries, concert venues, an aquarium, and so much more. Sit back on one of the many patios and watch the boats go by, partake in a cruise, or rent a kayak and wave back at all the people dining on the patios. Can't decide on the West Bank or East Bank? No worries; Metroparks now provides a free water taxi to shuttle you to and fro!

Music Box
Supper Club

Jacobs Pavilion
2014 Sycamore Street, West Bank of the Flats | www.jacobspavilion.com

Surrounded by spectacular bridges, a high-end residential complex, the historic Powerhouse, and the Cuyahoga River, Jacobs Pavilion is one of CLE's hottest spots for live music. Part of the Nautica Waterfront District, owned by Jacobs Entertainment, this fabulous open-air amphitheater not only showcases local and nationally touring concert acts but enhances the experience with great views of the river. Wave back at all the horn-blowing boats slowly drifting behind the back of the stage. And it's quite a show when one of those huge international freighters passes by the big top!

Watersports on the Cuyahoga River

Yes, the Flats are not all about eating, drinking, dancing, and entertainment. Watersport activity on the river has skyrocketed recently, thanks in part to all the new development along the Cuyahoga, significant improvement in the water quality, better access to the river, and the opening of several equipment rental locations. Most notably, Great Lakes Watersports has a fantastic rental facility between the Music Box and the historic Powerhouse. On any given day you'll be able to get out on the water on a single or double kayak, Jet Ski, stand-up paddleboard, rowboat, pontoon boat, or a paddle boat and happily make your way up and down the scenic Cuyahoga.

NO. 43

Celebrate women's contributions in space at the International Women's Air & Space Museum

The International Women's Air & Space Museum
1501 North Marginal Road, Burke Lakefront Airport | www.iwasm.org

Located in Burke Lakefront Airport, this intriguing museum preserves the history of women in aviation and documents their continuing contributions to aerospace. It is the only museum of its kind in the world, displaying interesting artifacts, wonderful photographs, historic aviation inventions, authentic uniforms donated by the women who wore them, and other memorabilia representing women pilots, mechanics, mission controllers, and astronauts. Aviation legends such as Amelia Earhart, Sally Ride, and Bessie Coleman, along with many others who made an impact in air and space, all are honored throughout the concourse. Take flight and have a look!

NO. 44

Spread out on a blanket and have a picnic under the cherry blossoms at Brookside Park

Cherry Grove Picnic Area
3900 John Nagy Blvd., Brookside Reservation | www.clevelandmetroparks.com/parks/visit/parks/brookside-reservation

There really is no need to travel to Japan or Washington, DC, to experience the beauty of the annual cherry tree bloom. Just make your way down to Brookside Reservation, where each spring you'll find more than a hundred Yoshino cherry trees displaying their vibrant pinkish-white flowers. Planted in the 1990s, these flowering gems were gifted to the citizens of Cleveland from the Japanese Association of Northeast Ohio. Spread out a blanket, walk your dog, or just stop by to stretch your legs under these exquisite trees that stand to symbolize beauty, renewal, and change.

NO. 45

Navigate the forest canopy via zip lines and suspended bridges at Go Ape Zipline & Adventure Park

Go Ape Zipline & Adventure Park
16200 Valley Parkway, Strongsville | www.goape.com

Get ready for a daring outdoor adventure—it's time to Go Ape! With five action-packed treetop obstacle crossings and seven breathtaking zip lines, this aerial wonderland in Strongsville's Mill Stream Run Reservation will have you yelling like Tarzan. When you're not speeding by on a zip line, you'll be trying to keep your balance on suspended bridges and other high-rope challenges. The park also offers outdoor ax throwing. So when you are finally back on the ground, check out a hatchet and try to hit the bull's-eye.

Go Ape!
TREETOP
ADVENTURE
CHECK-IN HERE
OPEN
chimpanzee
LIVE LIFE

NO. 46

Let the kids run wild on all the iconic amusement rides at Memphis Kiddie Park

Memphis Kiddie Park
10340 Memphis Avenue, Brooklyn | www.memphiskiddiepark.com

Oh, to be a kid again! Memphis Kiddie Park, a true CLE landmark, is an amazing old-school amusement park built for children under 50 inches tall. Opened in 1952, the family-run park features eleven superbly maintained rides that are all classics from the early 1950s. Kids can take a seat on the Big Creek & Memphis Railway, ride a wooden horse on an original Allen Herschel merry-go-round, or buckle in on the Little Dipper, remarkably the oldest continuously functioning steel coaster in North America! There is no entrance fee, parking is free, and each ride is just one ticket!

NO. 47

Have your picture taken with one of the strategically placed Cleveland script signs

Cleveland Script Signs
Various locations throughout Cleveland | www.thisiscleveland.com/blog/picture-this

Created by Destination Cleveland, our city's wonderful convention and visitor bureau, the iconic script signs have become an attraction unto themselves. They're installed with scenic backgrounds and perfect for group photo ops, and you can find the signs at six different locations. Expect a short line at the Edgewater Park site, where the spectacular CLE skyline and Edgewater Beach are in the background. Other locations include Abbey Road in Tremont, the East 9th Street pier, Euclid Beach, Cleveland Hopkins International Airport, and behind the Foundry on Columbus Road.

NO. 48

Shop the Old World grocery stands for produce, meats, and bakery at the historic West Side Market

West Side Market
1979 West 25th Street, Ohio City | www.westsidemarket.org

Built in 1912, the West Side Market, with its famed yellow-brick Market Hall and 137-foot clock tower, is one of Cleveland's most treasured attractions. Listed on the National Register of Historic Places, this European-style market is visited by more than a million shoppers every year. Over seventy individually owned specialty stands, most of which have been run by the same family for generations, offer everything from fine meats, colorful produce, fresh seafood, and artisan bakery items to cheeses from around the world, and so much more. And you haven't lived until you've visited Frank's Bratwurst in the northwest corner booth. Soft roll, sauerkraut, stadium mustard . . . it doesn't get much better than this!

FOSTER'S MEATS
1908
1917
JIM'S MEATS
PIZZA
EURO SWEETS
DIONNE'S POULTRY
THE HOME PANTRY

NO. 49

Cash in on the opportunity to learn about our monetary system at the Money Museum

Cleveland Money Museum
1455 East 6th Street, Downtown | www.clevelandfed.org

Located in the Federal Reserve Bank of Cleveland and guarded by two stone statues, “Security” and “Integrity,” the Money Museum’s mission is to educate the public on every aspect of our nation’s monetary system. Designed by the prestigious Cleveland architectural firm of Walker & Weeks, the building features a magnificent ornate lobby with Italian marble lining the walls and gold leaf on the ceiling. Take a self-guided tour featuring wall displays and interactive exhibits on the history of money, cybersecurity, and cash operations, or request a guided tour, which will include an insider’s view of the historic building.

NO. 50

Shock your senses and puzzle your perceptions at the Museum of Illusions Cleveland

Museum of Illusions Cleveland
186 Euclid Avenue, Downtown | www.moicleveland.com

Talk about flipping your world upside down! This mesmerizing museum on the first floor of the historic May Company building has over sixty mind-blowing exhibits that simply need to be seen to be believed. Opened in 2024, the 9,000-square-foot museum features illusionist rooms, optical illusions, unexplainable holograms, and a playroom with didactic puzzles and games. And you'll find great photo ops around every corner. Take a pic of your head on a platter, levitating over the museum's Euclid Avenue entrance, or hanging upside down from a basketball hoop. Just remember . . . nothing is ever quite as it seems!

NO. 51

Meet Lucy, our 3.2-million-year-old ancestor, at the Cleveland Museum of Natural History

Cleveland Museum of Natural History
1 Wade Oval Drive, University Circle | www.cmnh.org

If you've been to the Cleveland Museum of Natural History before, well, it's time to go again! Already considered one of the finest museums of its kind in North America, the museum has just completed a massive $150 million expansion and renovation project, reimagining its campus and all of its exhibits and adding new public spaces. A few of the many highlights include one of the most complete mounted sauropods on display anywhere in the world, a cast of the skeleton of the famous *Australopithecus afarensis* called Lucy (she died in Ethiopia some 3.2 million years ago), and *Dunkleosteus terrelli*, a giant predatory fish that swam in Ohio's ancient sea.

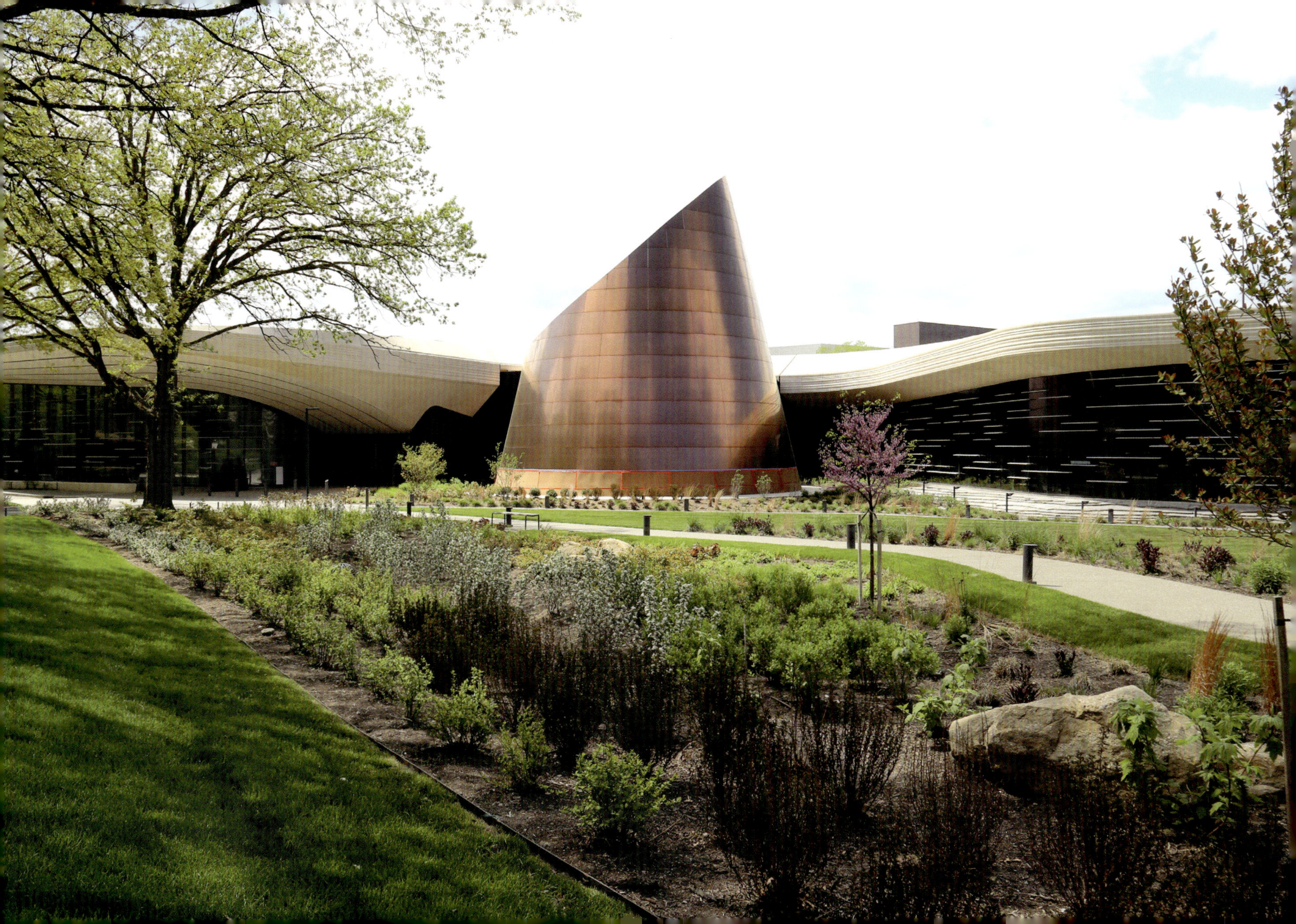

NO. 52

Splurge on a luxurious dining experience at the exquisite Marble Room Steak & Raw Bar

Marble Room Steaks & Raw Bar
623 Euclid Avenue, Downtown | www.marbleroomcle.com

If you have that certain milestone you are looking to celebrate, look no further than the Marble Room. It's rated as one of Cleveland's favorite places to dine, and the opulence of the stately room alone is worth the pricey check. Housed in the historic National City Bank building, which was constructed in 1893, the room is surrounded by 35-foot pink-marble Corinthian columns and topped with an elegant gilded ceiling. The menu is just as impressive, with plenty of high-quality seafood, a raw bar complete with caviar, and in-house dry-aged steaks, including a 42-ounce long-bone tomahawk currently priced at 135 bucks!

NO. 53

Relive the long history of local law enforcement at the Cleveland Police Museum

Cleveland Police Museum
1300 Ontario Street, Downtown | www.clevelandpolicemuseum.org

Clevelanders are so fortunate to have one of the few real police museums in the country. Located in the Justice Center, this wonderful museum is packed with photos, scrapbooks depicting notorious crimes, old police blotters, and lots of fascinating exhibits. Displays include an electric chair used by the State of Ohio (along with photos of the first ten people to be executed), the plaster death masks created to help solve the famous Torso Murders, and an actual jail cell you can sit in and have your picture taken. And vowing never to forget them, the Fallen Officers Exhibit solemnly honors the men and women who have lost their lives in the line of duty.

NO. 54

Interact with cutting-edge artistry at the Museum of Contemporary Art Cleveland

Museum of Contemporary Art Cleveland
11400 Euclid Avenue, Uptown | www.mocacleveland.org

Wow! The building that houses this museum is a masterful, 34,000-square-foot gemlike structure that is a dynamic visual work of art in itself. Clad in black Rimex stainless steel, it projects a mirrorlike reflection that changes its appearance depending on the time of day and the weather. Step inside this admission-free gallery and you'll be introduced to four floors of innovative paintings, drawings, modern sculptures, photography, and amazing video displays. And return often, because moCa is a non-collecting institution, with pioneering new exhibits being introduced three times a year.

NO. 55

Try not to shoot your eye out with a BB gun at The House from *A Christmas Story*

The House from *A Christmas Story*
3159 West 11th Street, Tremont | www.housefromachristmasstory.com

Carefully restored to its original cinematic glory, The House from *A Christmas Story* is definitely one of those CLE bucket list items. Guided tours through the shrine to the 1983 holiday classic filmed in Cleveland run every half hour. Just across the street is a nifty museum filled with hundreds of behind-the-scenes photos, original props and costumes, toys from the Higbee's store window, and even the family car. There's also a gift shop down the block where you can splurge on a Major Award Leg Lamp. And for those diehard *Christmas Story* fans, the entire house is available for overnight rentals.

NO. 56

Explore the rich firefighting history of northeastern Ohio at the Western Reserve Fire Museum

The Western Reserve Fire Museum and Education Center
310 Carnegie Avenue, Downtown | www.wrfmc.com

Opened in 2017 in the former fire station #28, this quaint but educational museum is dedicated to preserving the firefighting history of the eleven counties of the Western Reserve. Celebrating the contributions of local firefighters, the museum displays photographs, documents, early fire buckets and hoses, and antiquated fire alarm systems. The building brims with artifacts, but the main attraction is the large center room filled with exquisitely preserved vintage firefighting vehicles and equipment. Check out the Station 28 Kids Korner, which is a play area that lets the little ones dress up in fire gear, color artwork, and post their creations on the bulletin board.

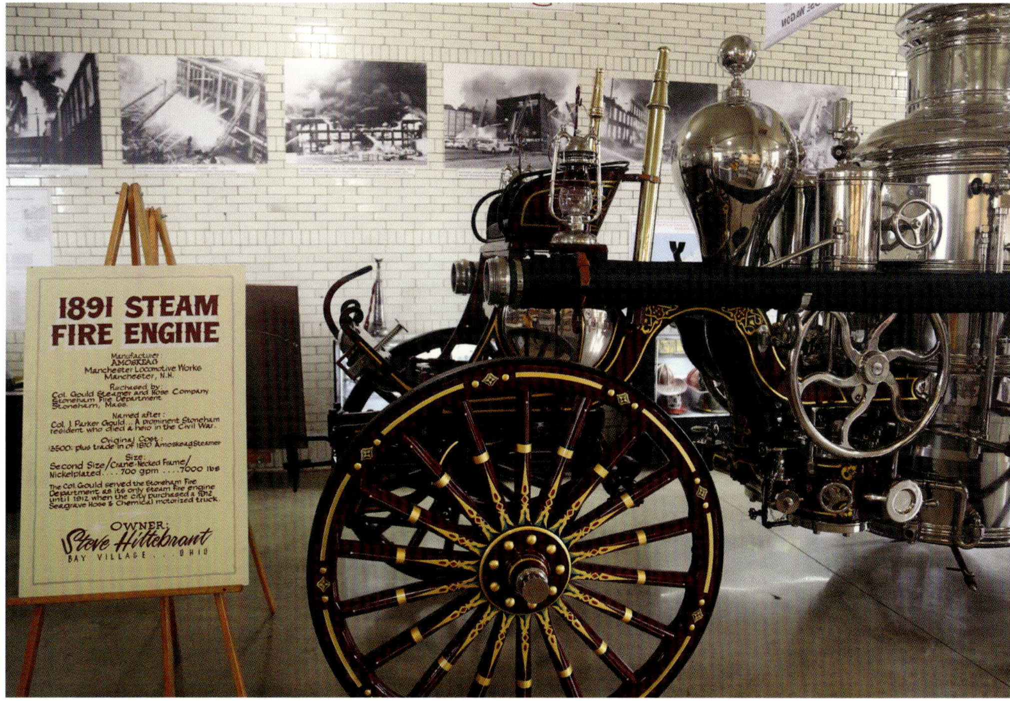

NO. 57

Join the greatest fans in the world and cheer on the home team at a major league sporting event

Cleveland Browns, Cleveland Cavaliers, and Cleveland Guardians
Huntington Bank Field, Rocket Arena, and Progressive Field | www.clevelandbrowns.com, www.nba.com/cavaliers, www.mlb.com/guardians

You don't have to be from CLE to know that Cleveland has some of the best, loudest, and most loyal sports fans in the world. Winning or losing, scores of enthusiastic loyalists consistently pack the Dawg Pound to bark for the Browns, sell out the Arena to cheer on the Wine and Gold, or fill the stands at the corner of Carnegie and Ontario to scream and shout for the Guards to pull off some late-inning heroics. The CLE lives and dies with our Brownies, Cavs, and Guards, and there is no better place to be than in the stands when the home team is in town. Woof, woof!

PROGRESSIVE
meijer
OPENING DAY 2024
PROGRESSIVE
BLASTER
PHANTOM FIREWORKS
SHERWIN-WILLIAMS
PEPSI
UNIONHOME MORTGAGE
bet365
DollarBank
PROGRESSIVE

NO. 58

Attend an extraordinary, socially relevant, cutting-edge production at Cleveland Public Theatre

Cleveland Public Theatre
6415 Detroit Avenue, Gordon Square | www.cptonline.org

With a focus on developing and producing original plays and interpreting classic works that are experimental in form and socially conscious in content, Cleveland Public Theatre has garnered an international reputation as a premier professional alternative theater. Founded in 1981, CPT has expanded to include two internal performance companies, the Latino-inspired Teatro Público de Cleveland and the Arabic-speaking Masrah Cleveland Al-Arabi. The theater is also known for presenting free community events, educational programs, and, with a focus on making theater as accessible as possible, a "Choose What You Pay" program.

Photo by Steve Wagner, courtesy of Cleveland Public Theatre

NO. 59

Get a bird's-eye view of CLE from the Terminal Tower Observation Deck

Terminal Tower Observation Deck
50 Public Square, Tower City Center, Downtown | www.terminaltower.com/towerlights

The hours are rather limited, and you have to buy your ticket online in advance, but once you reach the observation deck on the forty-second floor of Terminal Tower, the panoramic views of the city are phenomenal. No longer the tallest building in Cleveland, but easily one of CLE's most recognizable landmarks, the tower's circular viewing deck 710 feet above Public Square exposes the wild twists and turns of the mighty Cuyahoga River. You'll also get a bird's-eye view of all our major sports stadiums, a grand view of Lake Erie, and an aerial perspective of the wonderful renovations happening all around the city.

Photos courtesy of Amanda Chambers

NO. 60

Enjoy internationally acclaimed musicians presented at no cost by CityMusic Cleveland

CityMusic Cleveland Chamber Orchestra
Various Locations Throughout NE Ohio | www.citymusiccleveland.org

Cleveland is blessed with an abundance of opportunities to experience the arts, but none may be as creative and gratuitous as CityMusic Cleveland. Featuring a schedule comprising both chamber music (with a smaller body of players) and the larger orchestral performances, the classical-music presentations are often accompanied by exhibits of local artwork and are always free to the public! Performed in a variety of different community venues, CityMusic hopes to bring people of all walks of life together, especially those who haven't been to an orchestra concert before.

NO. 61

Explore the CLE's oldest structure on its original site at the Dunham Tavern Museum

Dunham Tavern Museum & Gardens
6709 Euclid Avenue, Midtown |
www.dunhamtavern.org

Located along the old Buffalo-Cleveland-Detroit Post Road, which is now Euclid Avenue, the 1824 home of Rufus and Jane Pratt Dunham is the oldest building still standing on its original site in the city limits of Cleveland. The colonial farmhouse, which was enlarged by the Dunhams in 1840 to include a taproom and sleeping quarters for stagecoach drivers, has two wonderfully preserved floors to explore, offering the opportunity to glimpse into the daily lives of early Greater Cleveland settlers and explorers. Behind the main residence you will find a rebuilt barn, which hosts events and celebrations, a log cabin structure where the Dunhams lived until the main structure was built, the gardens, and an existing orchard.

DUNHAM
Tavern Museum
1824

NO. 62

Step back in time at the fully restored Victorian shopping village of Grand Pacific Junction

Grand Pacific Junction
Williams Way & Columbia Road, Olmsted Falls | www.grandpacificjunction.com

Tucked away in quaint Olmsted Falls is Grand Pacific Junction, a historic hidden treasure lined with red-brick sidewalks and filled with over thirty specialty shops, all located in buildings dating to the mid-1800s. You can enjoy afternoon high tea at Clementine's, purchase handcrafted goods in the original jailhouse, get a haircut in an old-fashioned barber shop, and scrounge for antiques in the Treasure House of the Falls. After strolling the village, cross over the railroad tracks to admire the covered bridge, then stop into Moosehead Hoof & Ladder, housed in a historic 1940 firehouse overlooking the river below, for a bite to eat.

NO. 63

Get in line for a famous corned beef sandwich at Slyman's Restaurant and Deli

Slyman's Restaurant and Deli
3106 St. Clair Avenue, Goodrich Kirtland | www.slymans.com

Drive down St. Clair Avenue and it's easy to find . . . just look for the line! Clevelanders in the know have been queuing to get into this modest, unpretentious deli for decades. And although there are plenty of items on the menu, most are in line waiting for their chance to gobble up what most consider the biggest and best corned beef sandwich in town. No need to travel to NYC for an authentic New York–style deli experience, we have it right here in the best location in the nation.

NO. 64

Share in the fascinating history and culture of the Ukrainian people at the Ukrainian Museum

Ukrainian Museum–Archives
1202 Kenilworth Avenue, Tremont | www.umacleveland.org

Founded in 1952 by Leonid Bachynsky, a Ukrainian native living in Cleveland, the Ukrainian Museum–Archives contains one of the largest collections of materials pertaining to Ukrainian culture and immigration in North America. Recognized internationally, the museum houses over 20,000 books, thousands of newspapers, photographs, folk costumes, arts and crafts, sheet music, works of fine art, and their famous *pysanky* (Ukrainian Easter eggs). Be sure to check out the recently opened annex behind the main building, which holds a gallery for special exhibitions.

Слава Україні
Героям Слава

NO. 65

Try to find the hidden entrance to one of Cleveland's notorious speakeasies

Velvet Tango Room
2095 Columbus Road, Duck Island |
www.velvettangoroom.com

You may have already been to the Velvet Tango Room for a sophisticated cocktail, or to listen to the live jazz soulfully resounding throughout the swanky lounge. But have you entered the closet door next to the baby grand piano? Step inside and pull on one side of the floor-to-ceiling framed mirror on the back wall. Voilà! And you thought the front space was posh! Now go back into the front room, grab your friends and cocktails, and have a seat in one of CLE's favorite hidden speakeasies.

Quintana's Barber & Dream Spa
2200 South Taylor Road, Cleveland Heights | www.qbds.net/speakeasy

Wow. Now this gem is a speakeasy! Begin by walking up the porch steps and entering Quintana's Barber Shop, where regular customers sit in vintage barber chairs enjoying an old-fashioned straight razor shave or trim. Just to your right, climb a few stairs and you'll find a bookcase stacked with novels. Open the correct book and press the green button, and the entire bookcase swings open to reveal a gorgeous wood-trimmed speakeasy with plush leather seats, dim lighting, and one of the finest whiskey selections in the city. It doesn't get much better than this!

CLASSICS CONT...
12
OLD FASHIONED
GOLD RUSH
15
BOULEVARDIER
DARK & STORMY
WHISKEY SOUR
16
MORNING GLORY FIZZ

NO. 66

Find yourself in the money after wagering on the trotters at Northfield Park

Northfield Park Racetrack
10705 Northfield Road, Northfield | www.mgmnorthfieldpark.mgmresorts.com/en/racetrack.html

Ladies and gentlemen . . . place your bets! The trotters have been running year-round at this half-mile oval since 1957, and now that this storied racetrack has been remodeled with a Vegas-style betting lounge and simulcast racing being broadcast live from tracks across America, the old gal looks better than ever. Put $2.00 down on your favorite horse and shimmy up close along the rail, or have a seat and cheer your horse on in the glass-enclosed grandstand. And look at it this way: if you lose at the track, you can always go next door to the MGM casino and win it all back!

NO. 67

Get inspired by marveling at all the restored religious statues at the Sanctuary Museum

The Sanctuary Museum
12905 Madison Avenue, Birdtown
www.thesanctuarymuseum.org

Housed in former Saint Hedwig's Church, which was built in 1905 to serve the area's Polish immigrants, the Sanctuary Museum lovingly preserves and restores religious statues, exquisite art, and artifacts of the Catholic faith. This captivating gallery is packed with reliquaries, chalices, statues, and an unbelievable collection of stained-glass windows, most of which have been rescued from closed parishes in the CLE area. The Holy Family statue from Saint Procop Church, a Franz Thaddeus Lang Chalice, the Young Jesus in the Temple, and the oldest artifact found in the museum, Our Lady of Perpetual Help, dating to 1855, are just a few of the amazing items on display.

NO. 68

This is Cleveland, baby . . . so rock the night away at CLE's celebrated clubs and ballrooms

The Grog Shop
2785 Euclid Heights Blvd., Coventry | www.grogshop.gs

Cleveland rocks! So it's no surprise that this is where you'll find some of the finest music halls in the country. One such place is the iconic Grog Shop, in the bohemian Coventry neighborhood, which has been featuring the best of up-and-coming local and national acts since 1992. Occupying the first floor, with the BSide Lounge in the basement, this cozy venue is the place to be to witness small-hall rock, cutting-edge electronic, hip-hop, metal, hardcore, reggae, and more.

The Agora Theatre and Ballroom
5000 Euclid Avenue, Midtown | www.agoracleveland.com

The legendary Cleveland Agora, previously on East 24th Street, where it would evolve as *the* premier concert club in the country, now resides in the space once occupied by the old WHK radio studios and auditorium. Look to this historic, old-school theater for performances by local bands, new musical trends, and some of the best world-class national artists touring today. Rock on, Agora!

Photos courtesy of Evan Duly

The Beachland Ballroom and Tavern
15711 Waterloo Road, Waterloo Arts District | www.beachlandballroom.com

Created by owners Cindy Barber and Mark Leddy in 2000, the Beachland has grown to become a pillar of the northeastern Ohio music scene. With two separate stages—the larger Ballroom stage in one space and an intimate Tavern stage in another—local and national touring acts can be found performing almost every night of the week. Some of the biggest bands in music, such as the Black Keys, Los Lobos, the Cramps, and the Dead Boys, have graced the stage of the Beachland.

The Winchester Music Tavern
12112 Madison Avenue, Birdtown | www.thewinchestermusictavern.com

With their main concert hall tucked away in the rear of the building and occasional musical performances in the smaller bar area, you'll find a slew of assorted genres performing on any given night at this popular Lakewood tavern. Some of CLE's best cover bands, punk acts, acoustic duos, drag performers, upcoming singer-songwriters, jazz groups, and veteran rockers all have honed their skills at this lively old-school tavern, which is also blessed with a very cool street-side outdoor patio and a wonderful, vegan-friendly menu.

NO. 69

Learn about the unique art of papermaking, letterpress, and bookbinding at Morgan Conservatory

Morgan Conservatory
1754 East 47th Street, Midtown | www.morganconservatory.org

Dedicating itself to the fine art of producing paper by hand, the Morgan Conservatory has keenly transformed a former machine shop into a multifaceted art facility, producing some of the finest handmade papers in the world. It's open to the public, and you'll experience a working studio that is jam-packed with letterpresses, artists' tables, and papermaking equipment. Behind the conservatory you'll find a unique Japanese kozo (mulberry) tree grove used to grow fiber for making specialized paper. Stop by their intimate paper store, where a full line of high-quality handmade papers are available for purchase.

NO. 70

Cross over the river on the historic streetcar level of the Detroit-Superior Bridge

Streetcar Level of the Detroit-Superior Bridge
Detroit-Superior Bridge, connecting Downtown to Ohio City | www.cuyahogacounty.gov/veterans-memorial-bridge

It's slated for year-round public access in the near future, and the first phase of the renovation of the lower streetcar level of the Detroit-Superior Bridge, officially known as the Veterans Memorial Bridge, is in full swing. Running under the open-air road traffic on the upper level, this fascinating tunnellike space is on course to soon become a public thoroughfare for cyclists and pedestrians. Luckily, city planners have opened up the architecturally impressive span for tours, art installations, musical performances, and other entertainment during special events and Take-a-Hike walks.

IRON CITY
BIKES
DREAM
TEAM

NO. 71

Cruise on over to the Crawford Auto Aviation Museum and relive the history of transportation

Crawford Auto Aviation Museum
10825 East Blvd., University Circle | www.wrhs.org/plan-visit/places-to-visit/crawford-auto-aviation-museum

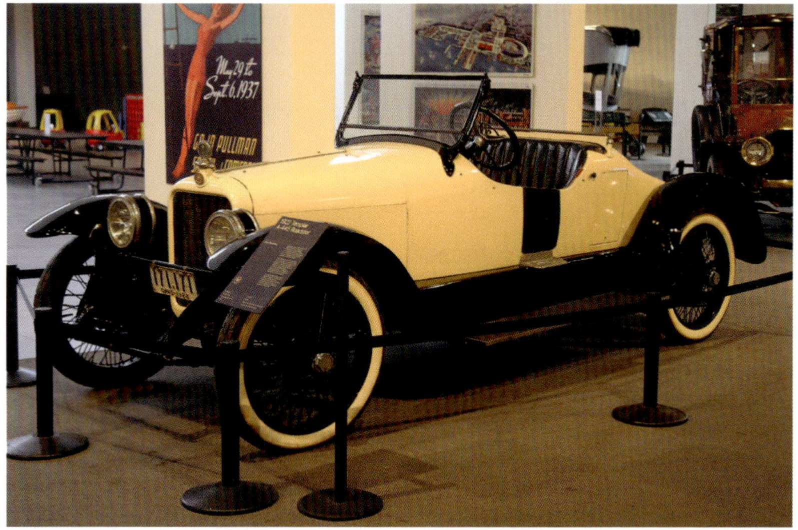

Founded by Frederick Crawford in 1965 and located in the Cleveland History Center, the Crawford Auto Aviation Museum is two sprawling floors filled with captivating transportation treasures. Although the museum's primary focus is automobiles, showcasing over 170 of the antique beauties, the collection also includes twenty-one non-car transportation artifacts (motorcycles, bicycles, and boats), twelve aircraft, and three remarkable carriages and sleighs. The museum, which began as Crawford's personal crusade to save historical vehicles from the crusher, also contains automobilia, including dealer brochures, parts lists, and owner's manuals.

G.L. HECHLER
PHARMACY
U.S. POST OFFICE

ROES
GUARDIANS OF CLEVELAND'S MOTOR HISTORY!
The city of Cleveland played a major role in getting America moving. This area has a more credible claim to being at the heart of the world's automobile revolution than anywhere else, save for Detroit. Alexander Winton, Walter Baker, and Rollin White were responsible for shifting Cleveland's transportation history from bicycles to automobiles, and established this city as a home for automotive innovation.
PEERLESS MOTOR CAR CO. CLEVELAND, OHIO 1905

27-078

NO. 72

Order up Cleveland's most authentic homestyle Polish food at the Little Polish Diner

Little Polish Diner
5772 Ridge Road, Parma | 440-842-8212

Located in Polish Village in Parma, this tiny yet highly acclaimed diner unquestionably provides hungry Clevelanders with some of the best traditional Polish cooking in town. Favorites such as pan-fried pierogies slathered in butter and sweet chopped onions, hefty stuffed cabbage rolls, and smoked kielbasa with sauerkraut are just a few of the menu items that taste just like they did in the old country. Everything is cooked to order, and the Little Polish Diner is carryout only, so it's best to phone in your selections before you arrive.

NO. 73

Wheel around the world's longest indoor MB track at Ray's Indoor Mountain Bike Park

Ray's Indoor Mountain Bike Park
9801 Walford Avenue, West Blvd. | www.raysmtb.com

Bike enthusiasts from around the Midwest flock to this massive indoor cycling paradise, the world's first and largest indoor bike park built exclusively for mountain bikes. Jammed with challenging trails and steep embankments perfect for getting you airborne, this pedalers' playground features areas such as the Jump Room (complete with a foam pit), the Trek Super Sport section, and the Pump Track. Take a spin around the Wildcat, ride over natural sections that consist of rocks and logs, or loop around on the world's longest indoor MB track, which is over a mile long. No bike? No problem. Just rent one of Ray's dirt jumpers and go at it!

NO. 74

Spend the day exploring sensational Cuyahoga Valley National Park

Cuyahoga Valley National Park
8000 Rockside Road (Independence) to Gorge Summit Metro Parks (north of Akron) | www.nps.gov/cuva/index.htm

Starting at Rockside Station and winding north–south along the Cuyahoga River and the Ohio & Erie Canal Towpath Trail, this amazing 33,000-acre national park is jam-packed with adventures. Join a ranger-led hike, kayak or canoe the river, visit a farm, explore the forests and wetlands, bike along the trails, or just sit back and marvel at the 60-foot-tall Brandywine Falls. Be sure to stop at the centrally located Boston Mills Visitor Center to check out the exhibits and get park info, and be equally sure to hop aboard the Cuyahoga Valley Scenic Railroad, one of the oldest, longest, and most picturesque tourist railways in the country.

6771
6771

NO. 75

Laugh your butt off at Hilarities 4th Street Theatre, Cleveland's premier comedy club

Hilarities 4th Street Theatre
2035 East 4th Street, Downtown | www.hilarities.com

Need a good laugh? Then head on down to Hilarities 4th Street Theatre in the Pickwick & Frolic entertainment complex on pedestrian-friendly East 4th Street. Developed by owner Nick Kostis, the festive facility includes Pickwick the Restaurant, Frolic Cabaret, a seventy-five-seat outdoor patio, and the main attraction, the four-hundred-seat comedy club, one of the largest made-for-comedy venues in the country. Lined with a mezzanine balcony with individual skyboxes, the comfy theater features the very best nationally known stand-up comics, local favorites such as Mike Polk, and newcomers looking for that big break in the biz!

NO. 76

Choose from fifty creative hot-dog toppings to go along with live music at the legendary Happy Dog

Happy Dog
5801 Detroit Avenue, Gordon Square | www.happydogcleveland.com

This famed hot-dog joint, which doubles as a live music venue, has been standing on the same corner of West 58th Street and Detroit Avenue since the late 1940s. Same original racetrack oval bar, same chrome barstools, same cramped booths. You can't help but love this place. And with more than fifty in-house-made toppings and sauces to pile on your wiener and tots, the menu card is as eclectic as the music. On any given night you'll hear rock, soul, punk, or polka from some of CLE's best local indie bands, cool regional groups, or national touring acts.

NO. 77

Discover a playground of science activities on the three floors of the Great Lakes Science Center

Great Lakes Science Center
601 Erieside Avenue, Downtown | www.greatscience.com

Opened in 1996, the 165,000-square-foot Great Lakes Science Center provides adults and children alike with three floors of hands-on learning experiences in science, technology, engineering, and math. The center contains hundreds of educational exhibits such as WindWorks, featuring an actual wind turbine, or the Polymer Funhouse, designed for future scientists under the age of seven. The main attraction just might be the NASA Glenn Visitor Center, one of only eleven such visitor centers in the country, where you can poke your head inside the actual 1973 Skylab 3 Apollo command module and also come face to face with a real moon rock from the Apollo 15 space mission.

GREAT LAKES
Science Center
NASA
Glenn Visitor Center

NO. 78

Partake in THIRD FRIDAY and experience four bustling floors of local artists at 78th Street Studios

78th Street Studios
1300 West 78th Street, Gordon Square | www.78streetstudios.com

It has been called Cleveland's best art event, and it happens every third Friday of the month in the renovated 1905 Baker Electric Motor Vehicle building. Today this mammoth warehouse is a wandering maze of award-winning galleries, art studios, and performance spaces. On THIRD FRIDAY they collectively throw open their workshop doors and fill every nook and cranny with authentic artwork, visual displays, designer furniture, arts and crafts, music, and eclectic cuisine. The monthly event is a feast for the eyes, ears, and tummy, as well as a great opportunity to interact with the artists.

NO. 79

Meander through towering trees and lush vines at the Cleveland Botanical Gardens' Costa Rica Glasshouse

Cleveland Botanical Gardens' Costa Rica Glasshouse
11030 East Blvd., University Circle | https://holdenfg.org/cleveland-botanical-garden

Home to a world-class collection of exotic plants and animals, the Cleveland Botanical Garden is another top destination on the north coast. You could spend the afternoon strolling the eleven different award-winning outdoor gardens spread out over 10 acres, but it's the 18,000-square-foot Eleanor Armstrong Smith Glasshouse you will remember the most. This centerpiece of a $50 million expansion is home to two separate climate-controlled ecosystems: the spiny desert of Madagascar and the Costa Rica cloud forest. With light streaming in from every direction, you'll be surrounded by towering tropical trees, hanging vines, and lush vegetation. Their avocado, papaya, and chocolate trees regularly bear fruit!

NO. 80

Plan a short getaway to the Shores & Islands and have a ball at Put-in-Bay and Cedar Point

Put-in-Bay
South Bass Island, western basin of Lake Erie | www.putinbay.com

Often referred to as the "Key West of the North," Put-in-Bay is one of the Midwest's favorite summer getaway playgrounds. Just an hour west of Cleveland and a short ferry ride from the mainland, this Lake Erie island is packed with attractions and activities for young and old alike. Take in the view from the top of 352-foot-tall Perry's Memorial Tower, tour the Heineman Vineyard, descend into Crystal Cave—home to the largest geode in the world, and explore South Bass Island in a golf cart. Best of all, just sit back and enjoy the drinks and live entertainment all along Delaware Avenue and the Boardwalk.

150 YEARS
1873-2023
BBC

BOARDWALK

National Park Service
U.S. Department of the Interior
Perry's Victory
and International
Peace Memorial

Cedar Point
1 Cedar Point Drive, Sandusky | www.cedarpoint.com

Cedar Point, on the shores of Lake Erie, arguably might be the most celebrated amusement park on the planet. Known as the "rollercoaster capital of the world," the park boasts eighteen amazing world-class coasters, including five thrilling rides that are over 200 feet tall. The park continues to expand and improve each year, adding the Top Thrill 2 in 2024, the tallest and fastest triple-launch strata coaster in the world! In addition to the sixty-nine rides in the huge 364-acre amusement center, Cedar Point also offers a mile-long beach with free daybeds, live performances and shows throughout the park, three separate kiddie areas, an attached marina, and overnight accommodations.

NO. 81

Begin your day with crepes, croissants, and an espresso at Le Petit Triangle Café

Le Petit Triangle Cafe
1881 Fulton Road, Ohio City | www.lepetittriangle.com

Opened in 2007 by Joy and Tom Harlor, this quaint and cozy neighborhood café at the intersection of Bridge and Fulton in Ohio City has all the trademarks of a wonderful little Parisian café: the intimate atmosphere, authentic French decor, and tables and chairs that spill out onto the street. The look might be reminiscent of Paris, but it's the food that will transport you there. Begin your day with Le Petit's sweet and savory crepes, fresh croissants, or fluffy omelets. In the afternoon you'll want to linger and chat over Coquille St. Jacques or Moules Mariniere with a glass of wine. And in the evening, their Boeuf Bourguignon is to die for. Bon appetit!

NO. 82

Spend a night singing the blues at the Brothers Lounge or House of Blues

The Brothers Lounge
11609 Detroit Avenue, Cleveland |
www.brotherslounge.com

While this legendary neighborhood lounge isn't all about the blues as it was in days past, when Robert Lockwood Jr. was somewhat of a regular and the likes of B.B. King and Buddy Guy would grace the stage, it's one of the few venues left where you can still find acts crying over a romance gone wrong. The entire space has seen renovations, and the acts on the main stage in the Music Hall are now more electric. So in addition to the occasional blues act or jam, you'll also find rock, jazz, reggae, and open-mic nights.

House of Blues Cleveland,
308 Euclid Avenue, Downtown | www.houseofblues.com/cleveland

Opened in 2004 in the old Woolworth's department store on Euclid Avenue, the House of Blues is part of a national chain of music venues that are rock and blues themed but also features all genres of music. The crowds usually line up early to see hip-hop, rock, pop, rap, jazz, and, yes, blues. A second entrance around the corner and smack dab in the middle of 4th Street brings you to a southern-inspired restaurant and a House of Blues gift shop.

Dan Bode
www.facebook.com/dan.mokobovo

I would be remiss if I didn't mention the legendary experimental blues artist Dan Bode. Dan has been on the music scene in CLE since 1981, and his distinctive gravelly voice and raspy tone perfectly complement his style of music—rooted in the blues and heavy on the harp. You can find Bode performing with groups such as Slideways, the Isolated Few, and Moko Bovo, and you can usually find the boys playing at the Millard Fillmore, as well as other local venues around town.

NO. 83

Shop for a print of a CLE landmark at the Paul Duda Gallery, or CLE apparel from Only in Clev

The Paul Duda Gallery
2342 Professor Avenue, Tremont | www.pauldudagallery.com

The Paul Duda Gallery, on the corner of Professor and College Avenues in Tremont, is the perfect spot for a CLE gift or memento. Opened in 2007 (the sister studio in Brecksville kicked off in 1990), this colorful gallery is stocked floor to ceiling with original works of art, most of which are fantastic cityscapes or iconic CLE landmarks such as the Guardians of Transportation, Progressive Field, the Rock & Roll Hall of Fame, and the Terminal Tower. The images are expressed in drawings, oil and acrylic paintings, photography, and giclée prints.

Only in Clev
17025 Lorain Avenue, Kamm's Corner | www.onlyinclev.com

Clevelanders *love* to wear apparel representing our grand city and our beloved sports teams, and the best spot to find this creative CLE-themed clothing is Only in Clev. Pick out a T-shirt, hoodie, or sweatshirt, then scan the walls covered floor to ceiling with hundreds of original designs saluting Cleveland, the Browns, the Cavs, the Guards, our neighborhoods, different nationalities, rock 'n' roll, and hard-to-find vintage images of local bars and restaurants. So many fun choices and different ways to exhibit your CLE pride. Only in Clev also has a nice selection of Cleveland-inspired head gear, glassware, signage, wall art, books, cards, and other CLE merchandise.

NO. 84

Marvel at the exquisite Victorian-era grandeur of the Arcade, "Cleveland's Crystal Palace"

The Arcade
401 Euclid Avenue, Downtown | www.theclevelandarcade.com

Opened on Memorial Day 1890 to great pageantry, "Cleveland's Crystal Palace," as it was known back in the day, was America's first indoor shopping center. Modeled after the Galleria Vittorio Emanuelle II in Milan, this iconic landmark is actually two nine-story office buildings connected by a five-story iron-and-glass roof, allowing the light to pour through, illuminating the elegant interior. The four floors of windows shine, the Roman mosaic floors glow, and those handsome balcony railings and mystical gargoyles appear to be shimmering in gold. Colloquially known as "the Old Arcade," this breathtaking esplanade was Cleveland's first building to be listed on the National Register of Historic Places.

NO. 85

Swing by Cleveland Rocks Climbing, where you'll find yourself reaching new heights

Cleveland Rocks Climbing
2831 Franklin Blvd., Ohio City | www.clevelandrocksclimbing.com

Located in the former historic Masonic Temple, down the street from Franklin Castle, you'll find this world-class climbing gym that offers unique opportunities in lead climbing, top rope, and bouldering. The 18,000-square-foot facility boasts three separate climbing areas designed for all skill levels and ages, complete with locker rooms and a workout area. You'll be able to challenge yourself on a diverse range of routes, with the tallest roped wall measuring a breathtaking 54 feet. A great way to safely practice your climbing skills before transitioning this exciting activity to the great outdoors!

NO. 86

Fill your cart at b.a. Sweetie Candy Company, the largest candy store in North America

b.a. Sweetie Candy Company
6770 Brookpark Road, Cleveland | www.sweetiescandy.com

Grab the kids by the hand, because you're about to enter candy paradise! This 40,000-square-foot mega warehouse is stocked floor to ceiling with classic candy, bulk candy, and boxes of wholesale candy. Everything from those hard-to-find childhood favorites to gourmet chocolates made in-house. And if all this delightful sweetness is not enough, the massive facility boasts a 150-seat ice cream parlor with thirty flavors of house-made ice cream. Better plan on spending the entire afternoon!

NO. 87

Ponder history from the iconic front porch of President James A. Garfield's Mentor home

James A. Garfield National Historic Site
8095 Mentor Avenue, Mentor | www.nps.gov/jaga

When Republican presidential nominee James Abram Garfield ran for the highest office in the land, instead of remaining in the background as candidates used to do, Garfield famously waged his "front porch" campaign from his home here on Mentor Avenue. The candidate openly invited groups of people to visit him here, where he spoke of patriotism and other important issues of the day. Today this magnificent farm is a National Historic Site, where you can take an informative guided tour of the home and walk throughout the surrounding property, which includes his 1880 campaign office, an 1893 carriage house, and a windmill.

NO. 88

Grab a table under a red umbrella and enjoy the band at the outdoor Whiskey Island Still & Eatery

Whiskey Island Still & Eatery
2800 Whiskey Island Drive, Edgewater on Lake Erie | www.whiskeyislandstillandeatery.net

Enter Edgewater Park from its eastern entrance off Memorial Shoreway and turn right (heading east) on the first road off the improved roundabout, and you will be entering one of Cleveland's more festive summertime playgrounds. Whiskey Island is where many go to enjoy Wendy Park or explore the historic Coast Guard station, but most are heading to party at the Whiskey Island Still & Eatery. Stretching along the marina and facing Lake Erie, the huge patio is packed with picnic tables topped with signature red umbrellas, and some of northeastern Ohio's best bands will help you dance the summer away!

NO. 89

Get the gang together and celebrate by cruising down the Cuyahoga River on a party boat

CLE Tiki Barge
1180 Main Avenue, the Flats | www.cletikibarge.com

Since 2020 the CLE Tiki Barge's BYOB excursions have been sailing within the inner harbor and down the Cuyahoga River. Their tiki-style boats, all topped with a signature thatched tiki roof, can accommodate up to forty-nine guests. The fleet is available for private cruises, but public sailings are also offered. So put a lei around your neck and jump on the *Original Tiki*, *Tipsy Tiki*, *Luau Lounge*, *Big Kahuna*, or *Extra Large "Party" Barge* and get ready to dance!

BrewBoat Cleveland
5300 Whiskey Island Drive, the Flats | www.brewcle.com

For something a little different, try pedaling your way down the scenic Cuyahoga River. BrewBoat's fleet features 31-foot-long catamarans that fit up to fourteen passengers, ten of which are seated on pedal stations around a central bar that powers a large rear paddle wheel. If cardio is not your thing, try one of the smaller pontoon party boats, where bike seats are replaced with comfy bar stools. In either case, look forward to doing what their motto says: Drink. Party. Float. Repeat.

NO. 90

Join in a game of volleyball, go for a swim, or just relax on the beach at Edgewater Park

Edgewater Park
Access from West Blvd. or Memorial Highway, Detroit-Shoreway | www.clevelandmetroparks.com/parks/visit/parks/lakefront-reservation/edgewater-park

A recreational staple in Greater Cleveland since 1894, Edgewater Park's 147 acres is now operated by Cleveland Metroparks, who have turned the lakefront property into a sparkling urban gem. Beautifully maintained, the park contains a sandy 2,400-foot beach, doggie beach, yacht club, fishing piers, volleyball courts, nature center, a huge playground with a separate toddler area, picnic tables and grills, jogging paths, and a $4.5 million beach house with an upper level serving food and adult beverages.

NO. 91

Raise your beer stein to an authentic Munich experience at the Hofbräuhaus Cleveland

Hofbräuhaus Cleveland
1550 Chester Avenue, Playhouse Square District | www.hofbrauhauscleveland.com

Jumbo pretzels with imported Bavarian sweet mustard, full-bodied lagers in giant steins, bratwurst and weisswuerste resting on a bed of sauerkraut, and musicians in lederhosen belting out German classics and rousing polka music. The Hofbräuhaus Cleveland, modeled after the legendary four-hundred-year-old drinking hall in Munich, will have you dancing on a table in no time! The venue opened in 2014, and the beer is brewed using original recipes handed down by the Duke of Bavaria and served in the same style of beer steins you'd find at Oktoberfest. Attend one of their monthly keg tappings or just wander into the dog-friendly German Biergarten, which holds over a thousand happy beer drinkers! Zicke Zacke, Zicke Zacke, Hoi Hoi Hoi!!

NO. 92

Take in a classic, foreign, or independent film at the Cleveland Institute of Art Cinematheque

The Cleveland Institute of Art Cinematheque
11610 Euclid Avenue, Uptown District of University Circle | www.cia.edu/cinematheque

Founded in 1986, the Cleveland Institute of Art Cinematheque, on Euclid Avenue, is respected as one of the top alternative film theaters in the country. It showcases exceptional classic, foreign, and independent films that will certainly be a CLE exclusive at the time of showing, since you won't find them playing in other movie houses in the area. Presented in the Peter B. Lewis Theater inside the George Gund Building, the three-hundred-seat auditorium features a 36-foot-wide screen, a 4K digital cinema projector, two 35 mm film projectors, and a 7.1 Dolby Digital sound system.

NO. 93

Explore the natural beauty of the eighteen reservations in the amazing Cleveland Metroparks

Cleveland Metroparks
Eighteen reservations encircling Cuyahoga County | www.clevelandmetroparks.com

Cleveland is blessed, truly blessed, with one of the greatest park systems in the country. Nicknamed the Emerald Necklace, a series of eighteen different park reservations covering an overwhelming 25,000 acres offer just about any kind of outdoor activity imaginable. Golfing, canoeing, hiking, biking, horseback riding, kayaking, swimming, birdwatching, fishing, and sunbathing are just a few of the many activities to enjoy. With ten nature centers, 325 miles of all-purpose trails, and eight lakefront parks, you may not have time to do anything else all summer!

NO. 94

Tour the final resting place of many influential Clevelanders at Lake View Cemetery

Lake View Cemetery
12316 Euclid Avenue, Cleveland | www.lakeviewcemetery.com

Designed after the Victorian garden cemeteries of Europe, Lake View Cemetery is a sprawling 285 acres of lavish funerary monuments, stately mausoleums, dramatic well-maintained landscapes, and winding roadways. This magnificent cemetery serves as the final resting place for numerous CLE notables, including the towering memorial tomb of President James A. Garfield, a 70-foot obelisk honoring billionaire John D. Rockefeller, and the jukebox headstone of Alan Freed. When visiting, be sure to step inside the Wade Memorial Chapel, one of the few remaining interiors in the world totally designed by Louis Comfort Tiffany.

NO. 95

Pretend you're a ninja warrior and challenge yourself on the obstacle courses at Adrenaline Monkey

Adrenaline Monkey
26800 Renaissance Parkway, Warrensville Heights | www.cleveland.adrenalinemonkeyfun.com

Did you ever dream of being on *American Ninja Warrior*? Then you are going to need a place to practice! This huge warehouse space is floor to ceiling with warrior obstacle courses, aerial rope courses, rock-climbing walls, monkey bars, and a lot more. And if your muscles get tired, take a little break in their game arcade. Bring the family, then sneak away to the second floor, overlooking the entire complex. That's where you'll find the aptly named Monkey Bar, serving cocktails and surrounded with large-screen TVs.

NO. 96

Leap around the CLE to marvel at all the mementos found here in Superman's hometown

Home of Superman
10622 Kimberly Avenue, Glenville | Other Superman mementos found throughout CLE

Yes, Superman was born right here in Cleveland. Writer Jerry Siegel attended Glenville High School in 1933, when he created Superman for the school's newspaper, and his best friend, Joe Schuster, who lived a few blocks away, generated the early drawings. The old Siegel residence on Kimberly Avenue is now a must-see attraction. Visitors flying into the CLE will find a marvelous Superman exhibit on the airport's lower level, and it's not unusual to find tributes and commemorative displays around town. Up, up, and away!

WELCOME TO CLEVELAND -
WHERE THE LEGEND BEGAN
SUPERMAN
"THE WORLD'S GREATEST SUPER HERO"
DID YOU KNOW SUPERMAN
WAS CREATED IN CLEVELAND?
SEE THESE SUPER SIGHTS IN HIS HOMETOWN

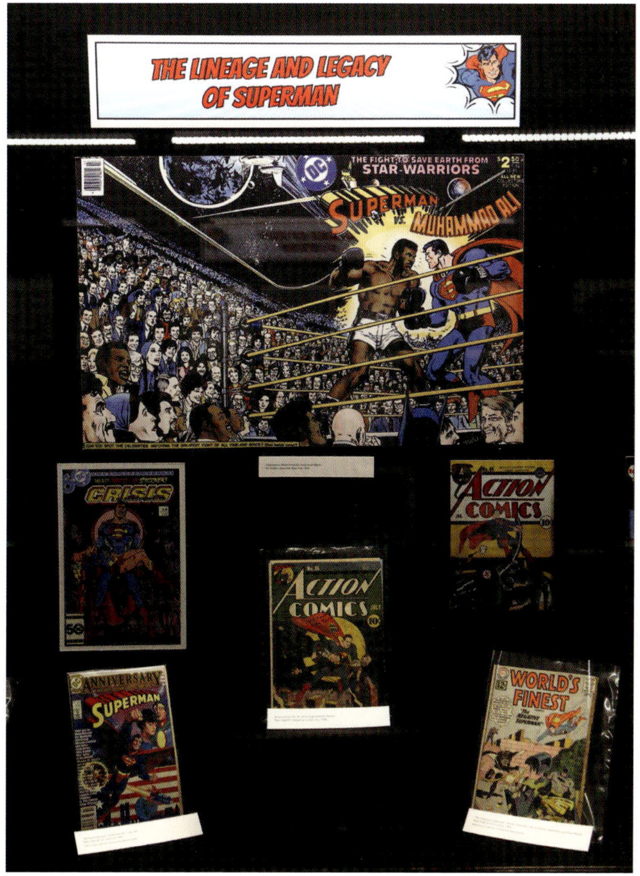
THE LINEAGE AND LEGACY
OF SUPERMAN
THE FIGHT TO SAVE EARTH FROM STAR-WARRIORS
SUPERMAN VS. MUHAMMAD ALI
CRISIS
ACTION COMICS
ACTION COMICS
ANNIVERSARY SUPERMAN
WORLD'S FINEST

NO. 97

Indulge in a world-class dining experience in the Parisian-like atmosphere of East 4th Street

East 4th Street
2015 East 4th Street, Downtown | www.east4thstreet.com

Nestled between Euclid and Prospect Avenues on pedestrian-only East 4th Street is Cleveland's newest destination for world-class dining, entertainment, and nightlife. The cozy red-brick lane, lined with outdoor patio seating and strings of lights dangling above, has been called a "prime example of 21st-century urban redevelopment" by the *New York Times*. Some of the CLE's finest eateries, such as Food Network chef Michael Symon's Mabel's BBQ or James Beard finalist chef Vinnie Cimino's Cordelia are here. After dinner, stop by the swanky Society Lounge for a handcrafted cocktail, or go see a nationally touring comedian at Hilarities 4th Street Theatre. And please remember to tip responsibly.

NO. 98

Relax with a botanical cocktail, coffee, or tea at Sacred Waters Kava Bar

Sacred Waters Kava Bar
15319 Detroit Avenue, Lakewood | www.sacredwaterskavabar.com

Looking to chill out with a natural mood relaxer? Then look no further than Sacred Waters Kava Bar in Lakewood. Kava is a root that originated in the South Pacific, where it has been used ceremonially for centuries. The drinks derived from this root reportedly have a medicinal quality that relieves stress and anxiety—in other words, they simply make you feel good. Belly up to the kava bar and try one of the café's delicious beverages that use herbs, botanicals, fruits, flowers, and spices. You're going to feel much better after you do!

NO. 99

Travel back to the mid-nineteenth century and experience daily life at Hale Farm & Village

Hale Farm & Village
2686 Oak Hill Road, Bath | www.wrhs.org/plan-visit/places-to-visit/hale-farm-village

Take a short thirty-minute drive south of downtown CLE and you'll find yourself in the mid-1800s at the remarkable Hale Farm & Village. Thirty-two historic structures, many featuring craft and trade demonstrations, are spread out over 90 acres of land that originally belonged to Connecticut farmer Jonathan Hale. Operated today by the Western Reserve Historical Society, the living-history museum uses period-costumed educators to deliver insight into daily life on the farm. Extremely skilled and knowledgeable artisans are on hand to demonstrate crafts such as glassblowing, blacksmithing, pottery making, weaving, spinning, and candle making.

GENERAL STORE
Wheatfield General Store
Reasonable Prices
GROCERIES
More and cheaper than ever!
We carry Pottery, Glass, Iron work, Textiles, Tin work & more!
Everything for house and farm
WE BARTER.
Credit Possible

NO. 100

Reserve a court and enjoy a beer at the Forest City Shuffleboard Arena & Bar

Forest City Shuffleboard Arena & Bar
4506 Lorain Avenue, Ohio City | www.forestcityshuffleboard

You might have imagined that pushing a few little disks (which the shuffleboard crowd calls biscuits) with a long stick was just for retirees in Florida, but not anymore. Forest City Shuffleboard Arena & Bar, in a spacious brick building near the western edge of Ohio City, has made shuffleboard the cool new thing. The brightly lit venue features five indoor courts, two outdoor courts on the patio, and two regulation shuffleboard tables. And not to worry if you have never played before—the staff is happy to explain the rules. Grab a beer and give it a go!

NO. 101

Watch a luminous sunset over Lake Erie on the Solstice Steps in Lakewood Park

Solstice Steps
14532 Lake Avenue, Lakewood Park | www.lakewoodchamber.org/discover-lakewood

With our north coast location right on the shores of Lake Erie, there are many good spots to sit and contemplate a sunset in CLE, but none quite like the spacious Solstice Steps in Lakewood Park. Rising 36 feet in elevation and curving around the edge of Lake Erie, the huge white concrete steps are laid out in a series of five tiers, each curved tier with four 21-inch steps separated by a comfy grass walkway. Featuring beautifully designed upper and lower promenades, the spectacular landmark faces the point on the horizon where the setting sun reaches its northernmost point during the summer solstice. Bring a picnic and enjoy the show!

101 THINGS TO DO

(IN A HANDY LIST)

For your convenience, here's a quick-look reference list of all the "things to do" in this book. Try to check off as many as you can as you explore the city. And keep in mind that the list is in no particular order. I haven't put the "best" things first; each is wonderful in its own right. Also, some of the activities may be weather permitting, seasonal, or held at scheduled times, so please check ahead for current updates and availabilities. I hope you get to experience all these wonderful things to do in "The Land," and I know you will enjoy each and every one of them as I have. So go ahead and start your adventure and have a ball discovering Cleveland.

1. Discover CLE's rich history from 1796 to the present at the Cleveland History Center.
2. Climb aboard the 618-foot Steamship *William G. Mather*, "The Ship That Built Cleveland."
3. Honor our local veterans who served in the Civil War at the Soldiers' and Sailors' Monument.
4. Take in a play at Karamu House, the oldest producing Black theater in the nation.
5. Have a drink at Moe's Tavern, the inspiration for Moe's on *The Simpsons*.
6. Experience the excitement of a Broadway show in the dazzling Playhouse Square Theater District.
7. Savor the beauty of the artistic masterpieces at the world-renowned Cleveland Museum of Art.
8. Fall in love with the restaurants and Asian specialty shops in CLE's AsiaTown neighborhood.
9. Examine the huge array of medical artifacts at the Dittrick Museum of Medical History.
10. Take three quick steps and a hop on your way to the Polka Hall of Fame.
11. Climb aboard the *Goodtime III* for a narrated sightseeing cruise down the Cuyahoga River.
12. Find peace through mutual understanding by roaming the Cleveland Cultural Gardens.
13. Stroll down the sidewalks of Little Italy, lined with old-school Italian eateries, bakeries, and shops.
14. Pay homage to the most popular sport in America at the Pro Football Hall of Fame.
15. Get an up-close look at hawks, snakes, and owls at the Lake Erie Nature & Science Center.
16. Attend a Video Game Symphony concert by one of the world's only orchestras dedicated to video game music.
17. Explore the sprawling gardens, trails, ponds, and forests at the massive Holden Arboretum.

18. Show your respect for all humanity at Maltz Museum of Jewish Heritage.
19. Admire the spectacular waterfall, grab some popcorn, and stroll the quaint village of Chagrin Falls.
20. Run the loop around Jesse Owens Olympic Oak Plaza, honoring track and field's greatest athlete.
21. Roll the dice, play the slots, and find yourself in the money at JACK Cleveland Casino.
22. Climb down the hatch and dive into naval history at the USS *Cod* Submarine Memorial.
23. Get an up-close look at sharks and other sea creatures at Greater Cleveland Aquarium.
24. Spend an evening playing as many games as you like at the Tabletop Board Game Café.
25. Download Destination Cleveland's Brewery Passport and enjoy the beer at CLE's finest breweries.
26. Take a swing at Cleveland's historic League Park and the Baseball Heritage Museum.
27. Take a spin on the extensively restored Euclid Beach Park Grand Carousel.
28. Indulge in some legendary sweet treats at Malley's Chocolates, Cleveland's premier chocolatiers.
29. Feed the giraffes and pet the goats at the Cleveland Metroparks Zoo & Rain Forest.
30. Explore the folk costumes and unique artistry at the Cleveland Hungarian Museum.
31. Enjoy a chef-prepared meal while sightseeing on the water aboard the *Lady Caroline*.
32. Ride along with a local comedian and have a hilarious time on the Funny Bus Cleveland.
33. Enjoy an extraordinary concert by the Cleveland Orchestra, one of the finest orchestras in the world.
34. Become spellbound by the extraordinary collections at Buckland Museum of Witchcraft & Magick.
35. Stand in line for a "scoop of a smile in a cone" at Mitchell's Homemade Ice Cream.
36. Immerse yourself in musical history at the iconic Rock & Roll Hall of Fame.
37. Relax among the exotic and native plants at the Rockefeller Park Greenhouse.
38. Trek the Towpath Trail, the amazing 101-mile pathway that follows the route of the Ohio & Erie Canal.
39. Follow the aroma into Farkas Pastry Shoppe and indulge on their creamy "Old World" napoleons.
40. Become a Pinball Wizard with the all-you-can-play arcade games at Superelectric Pinball Parlor.
41. Tap into the pure inspiration of soulful jazz music at the BOP STOP or the Velvet Tango Room.
42. Eat, drink, dance, and party along the Cuyahoga River in the bustling Cleveland Flats.
43. Celebrate women's contributions in space at the International Women's Air & Space Museum.

44. Spread out on a blanket and have a picnic under the cherry blossoms at Brookside Park.
45. Navigate the forest canopy via zip lines and suspended bridges at Go Ape Zipline & Adventure Park.
46. Let the kids run wild on all the iconic amusement rides at Memphis Kiddie Park.
47. Have your picture taken with one of the strategically placed Cleveland script signs.
48. Shop the Old World grocery stands for produce, meats, and bakery at the historic West Side Market.
49. Cash in on the opportunity to learn about our monetary system at the Money Museum.
50. Shock your senses and puzzle your perceptions at the Museum of Illusions Cleveland.
51. Meet Lucy, our 3.2-million-year-old ancestor, at the Cleveland Museum of Natural History.
52. Splurge on a luxurious dining experience at the exquisite Marble Room Steak & Raw Bar.
53. Relive the long history of local law enforcement at the Cleveland Police Museum.
54. Interact with cutting-edge artistry at the Museum of Contemporary Art Cleveland.
55. Try not to shoot your eye out with a BB gun at the House from A Christmas Story.
56. Explore the rich firefighting history of northeastern Ohio at the Western Reserve Fire Museum.
57. Join the greatest fans in the world and cheer on the home team at a major league sporting event.

58. Attend an extraordinary, socially relevant, cutting-edge production at Cleveland Public Theatre.
59. Get a bird's-eye view of CLE from the Terminal Tower Observation Deck.
60. Enjoy internationally acclaimed musicians presented at no cost by CityMusic Cleveland.
61. Explore the CLE's oldest structure on its original site at the Dunham Tavern Museum.
62. Step back in time at the fully restored Victorian shopping village of Grand Pacific Junction.
63. Get in line for a famous corned beef sandwich at Slyman's Restaurant and Deli.
64. Share in the fascinating history and culture of the Ukrainian people at the Ukrainian Museum.
65. Try to find the hidden entrance to one of Cleveland's notorious speakeasies.
66. Find yourself in the money after wagering on the trotters at Northfield Park.
67. Get inspired by marveling at all the restored religious statues at the Sanctuary Museum.
68. This is Cleveland, baby . . . so rock the night away at CLE's celebrated clubs and ballrooms.
69. Learn about the unique art of papermaking, letterpress, and bookbinding at Morgan Conservatory.
70. Cross over the river on the historic streetcar level of the Detroit-Superior Bridge.
71. Cruise on over to the Crawford Auto Aviation Museum and relive the history of transportation.
72. Order up Cleveland's most authentic homestyle Polish food at the Little Polish Diner.

73. Wheel around the world's longest indoor MB track at Ray's Indoor Mountain Bike Park.

74. Spend the day exploring sensational Cuyahoga Valley National Park.

75. Laugh your butt off at Hilarities 4th Street Theatre, Cleveland's premier comedy club.

76. Choose from fifty creative hot-dog toppings to go along with live music at the legendary Happy Dog.

77. Discover a playground of science activities on the three floors of the Great Lakes Science Center.

78. Partake in Third Friday,and experience four bustling floors of local artists at 78th Street Studios.

79. Meander through towering trees and lush vines at the Cleveland Botanical Gardens' Costa Rica Glasshouse.

80. Plan a short getaway to the Shores & Islands and have a ball at Put-in-Bay and Cedar Point.

81. Begin your day with crepes, croissants, and an espresso at Le Petit Triangle Café.

82. Spend a night singing the blues at the Brothers Lounge or House of Blues.

83. Shop for a print of a CLE landmark at the Paul Duda Gallery, or CLE apparel from Only in Clev.

84. Marvel at the exquisite Victorian-era grandeur of the Arcade, "Cleveland's Crystal Palace."

85. Swing by Cleveland Rocks Climbing, where you'll find yourself reaching new heights.

86. Fill your cart at b.a. Sweetie Candy Company, the largest candy store in North America.

87. Ponder history from the iconic front porch of President James A. Garfield's Mentor home.

88. Grab a table under a red umbrella and enjoy the band at the outdoor Whiskey Island Still & Eatery.

89. Get the gang together and celebrate by cruising down the Cuyahoga River on a party boat.

90. Join in a game of volleyball, go for a swim, or just relax on the beach at Edgewater Park.

91. Raise your beer stein to an authentic Munich experience at the Hofbräuhaus Cleveland.

92. Take in a classic, foreign, or independent film at the Cleveland Institute of Art Cinematheque.

93. Explore the natural beauty of the eighteen reservations in the amazing Cleveland Metroparks.

94. Tour the final resting place of many influential Clevelanders at Lake View Cemetery.

95. Pretend you're a ninja warrior and challenge yourself on the obstacle courses at Adrenaline Monkey.

96. Leap around the CLE to marvel at all the mementos found here in Superman's hometown.

97. Indulge in a world-class dining experience in the Parisian-like atmosphere of E. 4th Street.

98. Relax with a botanical cocktail, coffee, or tea at Sacred Waters Kava Bar.

99. Travel back to the mid-nineteenth century and experience daily life at Hale Farm & Village.

100. Reserve a court and enjoy a beer at the Forest City Shuffleboard Arena & Bar.

101. Watch a luminous sunset over Lake Erie on the Solstice Steps in Lakewood Park.

INDEX

PIZZA
1917
GUARDIANS

WATER
TAXI
JACOBS
PAVILION